CONTENTS

BAOR

Boobs Are OverRated

Diann Simon Pintacura

Three family members' lives changed forever with a cancer diagnosis for each of them within four weeks. This started as a blog to keep my family & friends informed of my progress, or the lack thereof. It's a tad irreverent at times but that's how my thought process works; I will find humor wherever I can. If you or a family member is diagnosed with cancer, I hope this book can help your perspective.

BLOG

Well, I wish I knew what I put on here at 4:00 this morning but here we go. Shortly after Christmas, we found out that a dear, young family member has cancer. I am not sharing that info as it is not mine to share. Last week, our daughter, Rebecca, was diagnosed with melanoma. I've been her Mom for 45+ years so I will share her information along with mine.

Rebecca's first appointment is at Karmano's Cancer Center in Detroit on Monday morning. Pete & I will be going with her & her husband, Barry. Before we go, I need to learn how to pronounce Karmano.

As you all now know, we found out yesterday I have breast cancer. I have an appointment on Thursday, 1/31, at Sparrow to meet with the oncologist/radiologist/surgeon. I've been asked how this was found, allow me to share.

I had a mammogram on December 28th which came back normal. It was the most painful one I have ever had & I actually called MSU to ask the name of the tech so I wouldn't get her next year. Anyway, my poor left breast was sore a few days later & I could feel - for lack of a better word - bumplies in it. I was actually thinking the mammographer had broke me. So, I went to my family doctor, she could feel them also & ordered an ultrasound. I had that last week, the bumplies are of no concern - basically old lady boobs. But during the ultrasound they found a lesion nowhere near the original area of interest. They did a biopsy this past Monday and we got the results yesterday. So, you now know what I know.

The only thing else to share is the dang dog is eating birdseed.

BLOG TITLE

The title of this blog is appropriately "Boobs Are OverRated".

TELLING MOM

OK, didn't sleep much Wednesday night so at 7:30 Thursday night, I told Pete, I have got to go to bed. So here I am wide-awake since midnight. I'm like a baby that has its' nights & days mixed up.

First of all, since some of this is going to be difficult to share without revealing the identify of my family member with cancer, I am designating that person with the gender-neutral name of Jordan.

As you already know, Mom was told about Jordan's & Rebecca's cancers within 3 weeks of each other. Just follow along here - part of Mom's Christmas gift this year is receiving a bouquet every month through June. Mom called me Wednesday (1/23) afternoon stating "I just received the bouquet from you kids, thank you very much, but I have to tell you this. It has two yellow roses! I have been praying for Jordan & Rebecca including prayers to St. Theresa. The bouquet has several flowers but only 2 yellow roses; it is St. Theresa's way of telling me she has heard my prayers and both of them will be ok.".

An hour and a half later, I receive my cancer diagnosis & one of my first thoughts was "Mom is going to have kittens" (no small feat since she had a hysterectomy 20 years ago). When we left Sparrow, I asked Pete to please stop at the florist nearby & I will get one yellow rose and that's how we can tell Mom that I, too, have cancer. Well - what kind of florist doesn't have yellow roses? They were out so I asked if they had white, she said yes & I said fine, I'll take a white one & please spray paint it yellow. (Hey, I spray paint chipmunks, why not flowers?)

My Mother is pretty astute so I figured when she saw me with a yellow rose, she'd quickly figure out what was going on. I over-estimated this a bit. We arrive at Mom's and before going in, I took off my coat (it was a balmy 28 degrees) and wrapped it around the aforementioned rose. We go in, chat a bit, and I told Mom I had something to show her & brought out the rose. She smiles from ear-to-ear, practically glowing; she sniffs this rose that smelled like an auto body shop and goes on to thank me for bringing another rose representing St. Theresa granting her prayers. Several thoughts run through my head within seconds, one of the printable ones "You've got to be kidding me". So, I went up, gave her a hug and whispered "I have breast cancer". The poor thing just about collapsed.

I told her we'd all get through this, I'm staying positive. I told her I had told God that I can handle cancer for me if He takes it away from my daughter so I'm ok with this as long as Rebecca's melanoma can be fully removed. She's pretty distraught and says "You can be positive, you don't know what it's like to have a daughter with cancer." I replied "Ummm, Mom, yes I do."

Mom doesn't get too emotional around us kids but for some reason can let go with my sister-in-law Pat (real name). After Mom heard about Jordan & Rebecca, both times she turned to Pat so we had already called & asked Pat to give us 15-20 minutes then please come over. Bless her heart for staying with Mom a while after we left to inform our son's family.

Before we left, Mom - she's not overly dramatic at all but she is struggling - said why can't God take me instead of putting this on my Grandkids & my kids. I hugged her & told her I didn't know but we aren't ready to lose her yet. Translation: "We apparently haven't yet made you miserable enough".

Please keep my Mom in your thoughts & prayers.

P.S. Mom has this little rodent dog called Mimi that literally weighs 3 pounds. Quite often this summer, I would pick Mom up to go somewhere so Mimi would need to go in her crate. After a few incidents of this, Mimi, who would typically run around my feet to be picked up, started running to her bed & curling into a ball facing the wall when I arrived. That dogs brain is so small she thought we couldn't see her thus no crate. The last 2 times we've been to Mom's is to tell her about Rebecca & my cancers. I'm thinking the next time we show up at Mom's, she's going to be curled up on the floor with Mimi.

TELLING YOUR IMMEDIATE FAMILY

This morning we will start with our dear daughter Rebecca. As you know, she received her diagnosis on January 17th. She and her husband, Barry, told their sons that night. Noah is 13, Gavin is 12. Noah said "That's depressing, I'm going to my room to cry". Gavin just said he was going to his room. My poor little dudes. We have her appointment at Karmano's Cancer Center tomorrow morning. It will be a relief to get a surgery date but my stomach is still in knots.

We learned about Jordan right after Christmas, Rebecca on 1/17 then here I come along on 1/23. We were all so stunned by two family members finding out they had cancer within a few weeks that when I told my kids & grandkids, the reaction was more "you have to be kidding". (Maybe they don't love me as much as I thought.....mmmm.)

Let me cut back to this summer a bit - obviously I'm not your average Grandma & so what. Noah, Gavin & I were going to play a game of Pig (you know, toss the basketball through the hoop, get a letter when you miss...). The boys being the age they are, seem to be fascinated with the word "Penis". We get ready to play "Pig" and Noah suggests we play "Penis". Without batting an eye, I said "Fine, after that we will play Vagina". We played Pig. While the young gentlemen are fine with tossing around the male body terms, they are not so fine with the female versions. Which brings us back to 1/23.

After receiving my diagnosis, we drove to my daughter's home in Howell to tell them. Of course the terms breast and/or boob were lobbed around. I finally said to the boys "I bet you never thought you'd hear breast or boob so many times in an hour". Noah replied "Grammy, it hasn't even BEEN a half hour". I called Barry's daughter Ellen, who immediately burst into tears; she'll get a hug when I see her later today (they all will).

My son's family wasn't going to be home till around 7:30 p.m. so we told them we'd stop by then. I texted our oldest granddaughter & asked if her & her husband could be at her Dad's at 7:30. She replied they are both tired & "unless it is life or death" we will pass. I texted back "See you at 7:30". Nothing quite like being frank.

We then stopped by Jordan's. There was no way I was sharing this news via a phone call, text, whatever with Jordan. We hugged a lot.

Today we were supposed to have a family dinner at 4:00 for January & February birthdays; I've been thawing a turkey most of the week. With the impending snow storm & Rebecca's 7:30 a.m. appointment in Detroit tomorrow, we decided to book a hotel for tonight in Detroit. Due to other obligations, we couldn't move the time up for today so at 4:00 we are doing cake/cookies/ice cream/gifts, booting everyone out by 5:30 and headed to Detroit. As for the turkey, I put it on Facebook to give it away & someone is picking it up shortly.

REBECCA'S APPOINTMENT

They did a full body check and removed one more 'suspicious' mole; results will be back next week. As to the earlier one, we received good news that only further removal of that area is required; no lymph node testing is needed. They will, of course, do testing on what they take out as well as send it to Castle Biosciences which will look at the genetics & predict future risk.

They will be removing the area around the first mole on Monday, February 18th. If the one removed today comes back the same as the 1st, they will remove that one on the same date. Thank you for your prayers & good thoughts for her; please keep them coming. She will have full body checks every 3 months for 1 year then every 6 months moving forward.

The doctor also said her immune system had started 'attacking' the first mole - who knew it did that? (rhetorical question only)

Everyone at Karmano's Cancer Center from the valet to the check-out person was very kind; I hope we only need to visit it one more time for their services but we were pleased with what we saw today. The snow in the Detroit area very thoughtfully held out till we were on our way home. A slow but safe trip home.

Hope everyone stays warm & safe.

INSULT TO INJURY

I have two huge cold sores on my lip that are just gorgeous. When I get to my appointment on Thursday, the doctors are going to say "Never mind the cancer, let's deal with those two huge blobs on your lip.".

WELL....

...here we go kids. My appointments start at 9 a.m., the last one today is at 1:00 p.m. I will update this with the results when we get home. Today, my daughter posted on Facebook "I am ready for 2019 to be done.". I replied "Be careful with that as I said the same thing about 2018 and look where we are now.". And it's only been a month!!! Yes, I know it could be worse so don't waste your time telling me that :)

POST-APPOINTMENT INFO (ME)

So, we spent all day at Sparrow starting at 9:00 a.m., get home to find 5 piles of loose dog bowel on the floor. Guess how the rest of the day went? :) :)

Actually, I am comfortable with our decision. We had 2 options: a lumpectomy with radiation or a mastectomy. Based on a couple of items, I have chosen to do a double mastectomy. First, a brief lesson on radiation of the breast: If a tumor is - say - at the top of the breast & is removed followed by radiation & the tumor comes back at the bottom of the breast, one can again have a lumpectomy followed by radiation. However, if it is centrally located, radiation is a one-time deal; if it came back, a mastectomy would be required.

This particular 'lesion' is small and is rated at only a 1. However, it is centrally located in my left breast, thus a one-shot radiation. I would rather have surgery at 63 than 73. BTW, a minimal amount of breast tissue remains after a mastectomy so breast cancer can recur but if it did, I could then have radiation.

The other factor is I had a 3-D mammogram on December 28th and this lesion was not found. If I did the lumpectomy, I would have mammograms every 3 months for a year, then every six months. I do not have any confidence that a second cancer would be found via a mammogram.

The surgeon, Dr. McKenna is on board with this decision. I had also previously chatted with my family doctor (the wonderful woman who ordered the ultrasound) & she thought this was a good plan.

Now, the kind of surprising portion of this is I am having it Monday morning (2/4); they had a cancellation in this time slot so there ya go. (Fellow shuffleboarders, I don't think Pete & I will be there Tuesday night.) I am feeling a bit rushed but that's ok. I have a Spring Break vacation with my kids & grandkids to get to the last week of March.

I'm trying to think if there's anything else to share & I don't think so. Well, maybe....at Sparrow when you are diagnosed with breast cancer, they have a 'workshop' where they present information on breast cancer, treatments, etc. There were 4 women & their spouses in this one. After the presentation, each couple is put in a separate room & the oncologists/radiologists/ surgeons rotate separately through each room. They then meet together & come back & make recommendations. This was all done well. At the presentation, a breast cancer survivor spoke and said if you have radiation, it is at the same time every day (M-F) and she stated she'd made a lot of friends during her 6 weeks of radiation. My heavens - AREN'T THERE EASIER WAYS TO MAKE FRIENDS????

Well, that's it for now. If anyone needs some extra bras, I'll have a few laying around.

1 YEAR AGO...

Today, my thoughts are with the Doerr family. Their wife, mother, grandmother, best friend, sister, daughter passed away in her sleep exactly a year ago today. The lives of her family & friends changed forever.

Everyone should aspire to be more like Lyn Doerr. Her life was not without challenges but she faced them head-on and most of the time with determination and a smile. Being with Lyn just made a person happy. Her laugh & her smile were contagious; a hug from her was really a true hug not just a perfunctory greeting.

Lyn was a shopper, not just for herself but her friends. I'm truly not much of a shopper & while in a store with Lyn, I did a lot of meandering. Pretty soon Lyn would show up with a few items - "Here, these look like something you would like." & she was right. When going to a store with Lyn, I don't believe I ever left empty-handed.

Lyn loved her family, her many friends, her pre-retirement job, and Bloody Mary's. It was enjoyable watching her mix her own Bloody Mary's at Leo's; it was truly an art form.

Lyn was the one that kept groups together, she organized gatherings, if she didn't see you that week, she would call to chat. She was in my life for only 12 years but she taught me a lot in that time; she's one of those rare people you meet & "click" almost immediately. I shake my head at the loss of her; it is still unbelievable.

When I say my night prayers & ask for special help for Jordan, Rebecca & others, I ask Lyn to help out with this. Even in death,

I know she will help.
I miss you, my dear friend.

Q AND A

Thank you to all who have shared their thoughts with us; it is truly appreciated & the support means the world to us. Below are questions I've received & my replies; I am sharing them in case you have the same questions. As you know I'm pretty darned hard to offend so if you have any queries, feel free to ask away.

Q: Why is she putting this on a blog rather than contacting us personally?

A: Because I have 60+ people to update & this is the easiest, most accurate way for me to do that. Pete & I welcome comments, messages, texts, phone calls, emails, personal visits, carrier pigeons bringing notes, etc. This is not to alienate anybody; it's just an easy way to keep everyone current while we travel down this bumpy, dusty, pot-holed, mud-puddled, curvy, log-strewn trail. Except for changing the time for the Christmas Day Gathering at my Mom's, I try to be flexible & consider everyone's wishes. This time, however, suck it up my buttercups, it is all about me.

Q: Did Pete help make the decision for the double mastectomy or was it a "My boobs, my decision" choice.

A: If it were up to Pete, I'd have three breasts.

-The serious answer is I have a lot of respect for my spouse & for whatever reason, he has the same for me. We make major decisions together, including this one.

Q: How do you get new skin? Do you need skin grafts to 'seal' the mastectomy incision.

A: I was going to ask you for some of your skin but I know you would only give it to me off your butt.

-The real answer is no; they stitch the skin together in what will hopefully be a nice, straight, pucker-free seam.

Q: Why did you decide to take off both breasts instead of just one?

A: If I'd wanted only 1 boob, I'd have stayed with my first husband.

-I did a lot of research on this & from those that had a single mastectomy years ago, the majority wished they had just removed both at the same time.

Q: You do realize you have to still wear a swimsuit top, right?

A: No.

Q: Are you doing reconstructive surgery?

A: Too old for that crap. I will have prosthesis which gives me a weapon to throw at people when they irritate me.

And a big thanks to our friend Jimmy Green for coining this " The Boob Blog".

REFLECTIONS

Some of you may be surprised to hear that I am not a very private person. Pete often says he doesn't have to tell anyone of the odd things that happen to me because I tell on myself first. How does someone come to willingly share information & to find humor in almost anything? Shitty life experiences.

Most of you know I was 17 & pregnant when I married one of the biggest doofuses in the world. I remember the night before the wedding, I was thinking very clearly "I don't want to do this" but for whatever reason I went through with it. Less than a year later, I had a baby daughter, was pregnant again & the doofus had taken off only to be seen in court when he was dragged in for non-payment of child support. So, I was working full-time and had two kids at 19. Not the worst thing in the world but I was ashamed of myself & embarrassed. I did not know anyone else who was divorced, there was still a strong stigma attached to that marital status. I did not like telling people the doofus had vamoosed; I felt it reflected poorly on me. Anyway, this finally began to change when I started a job at MDOT. My boss, a kind, very funny man by the name of Jim Dorr asked me about my family. I quietly said I had two children and was divorced. He replied "So what, it happens". I was like, " It does???". Anyway, I think that started me thinking I wasn't going to be embarrassed sharing anything again.

What really sealed the deal is when my kids let me walk through the Civic Center with about 2 rolls of toilet paper hanging out of my pants. I reasonably asked "Why didn't you tell me?". Their response "We didn't want to embarrass you.".

Just one minor example of finding an odd experience hilarious:

Years ago, there existed a Lime Green colored Cert; I believe the flavor was wintermint. It was a cold, winter morning as I was jauntily walking to work with a fresh minty mouth, courtesy of Certs. I was happily walking along and spied just ahead of me a gentleman from work who was slowly trudging along on his way to our building. I caught up to him at a corner just as the walk light turned to "Do Not Walk". Popping out of my mouth were the words "Lou, at this rate, by the time you get to work, it will be time to leave." As the gentleman turned to face me, I quickly deduced it wasn't Lou. I opened my mouth to apologize and popping out this time was my bright, lime green Cert which flew a short distance, adhering itself to the front of his black wool coat. That's me - classy. As we stared at each other for an interminable amount of time, the mint released its' grip and fell to the sidewalk between us. There were no words to be spoken. The light turned to "Walk" and I did just that - very quickly. As I approached our building, I was thinking thank heavens I don't ever have to see him again. As I waited and waited and waited for the elevator, guess who walked into our building & rode up the elevator with me. When I got off the elevator, I was laughing - how can one not? I could have been horrified or been ashamed but by that time, that ship had sailed.

I could also tell you about my eyebrows but that's a later story :). We are back to me not being a very private person. Ask me anything, I will provide an answer. If for some reason (can't think of one) that question offends me, I will let you know so we can discuss it. What was the topic of this? Oh yes...Reflections.

I truly do not think I have yet comprehended that cancer is existing inside of me. I sure as hell didn't invite it. It tried to hide from the mammogram but persistence paid off & it was discovered. (I might just throw a prosthesis at it later.) I guess I'm just numb. After Jordan's news followed by Rebecca's, I just cannot get my head around this. I wonder if I am jumping too fast into surgery on Monday but I don't think so. When faced with a serious problem, my first thought has never been "how did this happen", "who is at fault" or "woe is me". It's always been "Where do we go from here & what is the best approach to get there?". (Should have told THAT to my 17-year old self. But then I wouldn't have my son & his 4 daughters so I'm good with that.). Anyway, today I am chatting with a close friend & expressed my concerns that I don't yet have a handle on this & am proceeding haphazardly with lopping off some relatively precious anatomy in 2 days. She replied that I am very organized, always think things through & although I may not be aware of it, I've made the best choice using those processes. Patty - if you are wrong, you owe me a box of wine & a bag of BBQ chips.

Well, that's it for today. Love to all & as the saying goes....and to all a good night.

SUNDAY NIGHT

Feeling a tad apprehensive. So far, handling everything pretty well HOWEVER if the Super Bowl commercials suck, I will be upset!!!! They'd best not let me down.

PREP

First, this is the most boring Super Bowl game ever!! Not to mention, they are disappointing me with the commercials. Enough on this.

In 12 hours, I will be about ready to - as they say - go under the knife. Unlike a colonoscopy, the preparation is relatively easy. Go to bed, sleep, get up, take a shower.....which is almost exactly what I did this morning. I woke up, saw it was 5:30, told Pete "I forgot to set an alarm, it's 5:30, I have to take a quick shower & we need to be out of here in a 1/2 hour.". He asks what day I think it is & I realized it was Sunday. Oh - that reminds me; I've been asked what time the surgery is scheduled. We have to be there at 6:30 for an 8:00 'inject a needle into your left breast" then the surgery itself is at 9:30. The inject a needle portion is to insert dye to find the 'sentinel lymph node" so they can check to be sure there is no cancer in the lymph nodes. Geez, am I rambling or what?

Anyhow, there is some prep before leaving. Back in 1973, there was a lot of scuttlebutt about a book called "The Total Woman" wherein the author suggests women wrap themselves in Saran Wrap - or if you prefer, Handy Wrap - & greet their spousal unit at the front door. (Don't use the cheap dollar store plastic wrap or you'll just end up with a giant ball.) I have never read the book so have no idea what is actually in it but apparently a medical professional took the plastic wrap suggestion to heart. Tomorrow morning, I need to put a numbing cream on my left breast/boob/hooter/knocker/can/tata/whatever then put plastic wrap (we use Glad Cling Wrap) over it, put on a bra & proceed to the hospital. It's supposed to numb it so when they inject dye into it with a needle the size of my left arm, you aren't supposed to feel it. (Lot of 'it's in there but keep up & figure out on your own what is being referenced.) I personally think the dentist is probably still worse than this (I'll let you know).

Pete & I truly appreciate all the encouraging messages/emails/calls/visits/cards received and take strength from all of those. (I just had to wake him up - told you the game was boring.). Well, I believe I am procrastinating going to bed & lying awake till 5:30. No worries, I'll sleep most of tomorrow :)

Pete will update this tomorrow; I'd better still be alive or I will be totally pissed. Love to all.

SURGERY DAY

You will soon notice that is Pete and not Diann BUT Diann told me that I had to update her BAOR blog and for those of you that don't know me I do everything my wife tells me to do and for those that do know me I hear your snickers so as Diann would say "bite me".

We got here at 6:30 this morning for initial testing and surgery started at 9:00 and finished at noon. Dr McKenna said the surgery went well and they got to locate three sentinel lymph nodes they called hot. I knew if it had to do with Diann it would be hot! What that means is they were perfect to check for cancer. The initial test came back clear which great news. They will send the nodes to the lab for further testing.

She is still in recovery probably hiding from me because I can't see her until she gets out of recovery and into a room.

That's it for now.

DAY 0

Here's a 4 letter word you don't often hear from me: OUCH! All is good; painkillers & ice.

DOING WELL

First, really good news is Rebecca's second mole came back as negative. YIPPEE!! After her appointment on 2/18 to remove tissue around the malignant mole, she should be good to-go with full body checks every 3 months.

I am feeling fine; stitched up like Frankenstein. The incisions begin under my armpits which kind of surprised me but it's all good. There were 3 sentinel lymph nodes; the preliminary test of them was clear. They ship them out for further testing & we should get that news in a couple weeks.

This unit has double rooms; my first roommate was a quiet 99 year old lady who turns 100 in mid-February. Her bed was wired that if she gets out of bed, the 582 decibel alarm would go off. The nurses reminded her to push 'the button for the nurse" prior to trying to get up & they would help her & then the alarm would not go off. Apparently she heard "When the alarm sounds, push the nurse's button.". There was nothing to be done but laugh.

One of the staff said "OK we are moving her or you as you will never get any rest. So to quote Colonel Potter "Bug out". They moved me to another room & all is good.

The resident has been here & indicates as soon as the Doctor sees me, we can head home. Except for the underarm stitches, I feel pretty darned good. Hope you all have an excellent day.

HOME SWEET HOME

Well, less than 2 weeks after we were told I have cancer, the bilateral mastectomy is done & we are home. Can't move much faster than that. We will know by Friday if the lymph nodes he took are clear. That's all I have.

FORT

Or maybe a fortress. As a child (or maybe an adult), or with kids or grandkids, have you ever made a fort out of couch cushions & sheets? That's sort of what I am sleeping in at night.

I was given sound advice to either sleep in a recliner or get a wedge pillow for the bed. Opting for the wedge pillow, I also have a pillow under my knees (for my back), one on the wedge pillow for my head & one on either side of me for my arms for a grand total of five pillows. I feel like Carol Burnett in "The Princess & the Pea".

I didn't update this yesterday; I could have but was sort of in a pain-killer fog & was just a big blob most of the day. I've decided to do Tylenol during the day & the pain-killer just at night. Truly, except for where they took the lymph nodes & the areas near the drains, this is not as painful as I had anticipated. Until I sneeze, then that is definitely the worst. Frankly, I think sneezing is cruel & unusual punishment.

Pete is doing great helping me with the drains; I could do this myself if I had to but 3 hands work much better than 2 emptying these things. Since they didn't swap an extra arm for two breasts, I'm stuck with needing help.

I can finally shower today but have to wrap the drain hoses in saran wrap so I'm back to the Total Woman story - jokes on them, huh? I am doing my breast - or the lack thereof - exercises a few times each day. So, we're moving along.

Our family member Jordan & his/her physicians have chosen a chemo/radiation regimen and will set a date when to start that. Rebecca's excision is in 11 more days; will be glad when that is done & she is on the road to recuperation.

Thank you for your kind words & support. Love to all.

PRE-SHOWER

Hotshot here isn't as physically strong as she thought. By the time the drains were emptied, the bandages taken off the drain holes, the plastic wrap put over the drain holes, I was feeling pretty light-headed. Currently sitting down waiting for this to pass. Never thought of getting a shower chair......I will add it to a list for anyone else that needs to do this. Maybe I should just do what Marley's been doing - lay in the snow & wiggle around.

A COW OR A MAMA DOG?

Betcha that got your attention. I believe I mentioned I have 2 drains that go down a tube to their own little 'bulb'. The bulbs get emptied a couple times a day & we need to track the time & the amount emptied.

In the hospital, they pin the bulbs to the beautiful gowns. Prior to surgery, I was fitted for a post-mastectomy camisole. It's basically a vest that zips up the front & has two little pockets for the bulbs. Sounds like a great idea but to be honest it is uncomfortable as the dickens. The construction is somewhat stiff and I find it feels better to just pin the bulbs to the inside of the fashionable button down shirts I purchased at Goodwill. This morning I am walking down the hall & these bulbs, which need to be emptied, are swaying side to side. My thought: "My God, this must be what a cow feels like on her way to the milking parlor....or a mama dog with 8 puppies.". I should have had a clue because before emptying the bulbs, you must slide your fingers down the drains to empty them - they call it 'milking'.

The heck with all the info one can read about preparing for a mastectomy, I'm doing my own article :) Stay tuned.

IT'S NOT ALL FUN AND GAMES

Who knew, right?

The doctor assured Pete & I the results of my lymph node biopsy would be back by Thursday, definitely by Friday. Since we had not heard from him, I called Friday afternoon & were told the results were not yet back. Going to my reliable internet sources of The American Cancer Society, The Mayo Clinic, and The Cleveland Clinic, it was reiterated that lymph node results are back in 2-3 days unless additional testing is needed. Mmmm, someone forgot to share this possibility with us. I'm currently going with the ice storms delayed the testing; it closed schools, the State & County offices, it can delay lymph node tests.

For whatever reason, early yesterday morning was quite unpleasant. By 10:00 or so, things were back to whatever the hell is the new normal. My sister, Donna, and brother-in-law, Al came over & we had a good visit with them. Two naps later, our next door neighbors stopped in for a visit & the delivery of a bottle of wine. I'm not quite up for more than 1/4 cup of wine yet but it gives me hope that day is around the corner.

I've been getting by with a couple tylenol 2 or 3 times a day but early this morning said the heck with it & went for the pharmaceuticals. Areas seem to be getting a tad more sore as they heal. I am doing the exercises as directed.

On other notes of "interest":

A) I finally sold the quarter-sawn oak dining chairs we bought 9 years ago for more than a few hundred dollars; I replaced them

3-4 months ago with 4 antique oak chairs purchased for $70.00.

B) As many of you are aware, geez - in a nutshell, my son's ex-wife has 6 kids with 3 dads and after 12 years of effort, we finally accomplished getting all 6 kids away from her a few years ago (she is a drug addict). Well, guess who had baby #7 two weeks ago? Of course, the baby was born with drugs in its' system. Our granddaughter Alicia & her husband Evan, bless their hearts, are taking in the baby until a permanent solution is found. Evan & Alicia have our wonderful great-grandson Marshall who will be 2 in May & are expecting their equally wonderful son Harrison in late March. I hate to ask you for more, but please include them in your thoughts & prayers as they take on this unexpected, but loved, temporary family member & pray that the baby ends up in a safe, caring, permanent home. We are very proud of Alicia & Evan for taking this on; it isn't going to be easy. Pete & I hope to meet the young lady when she is released from the hospital & wish her well on her journey in this world. It is just my nature to want to help them but right now, I can't hold a cotton ball much less a baby or a toddler so settled with providing some "essentials" including a soft stuffed animal & a cozy blanket she can keep with her. Again, very impressed with Alicia & Evan; they are doing a very kind & generous thing.

C) I feel like we belong on Jerry Springer.

UNEXPECTED REVELATION #1

We are watching a movie & a guy (with a relatively flat stomach & a completely hairless chest - these 2 phrases are VERY important) is slowly pulling a t-shirt over his head. My thoughts? "Son of a gun, without the nipples, that is me!!!".

DEXTER AND A COUPLE OTHER THINGS

If you are familiar with the TV show Dexter, you will get this. If not, he wraps his victims in plastic wrap. To take a shower, my 'drains' need to be covered with press-and-seal plastic wrap. Pete has been putting the wrap on my sides; he claims he feels like Dexter. I lock him out of the bathroom � �

I am feeling more awake & have not had 2 naps during the day since Friday. My chest seems to be contracting and feels like I am wearing the world's tightest underwire bra; talked with the doctor & he's not concerned. I'm like WTH, a huge benefit of this was no more bras & I feel like I'm wearing the worst one ever made. This side effect better pass or I'm asking for my boobs back.

As previously stated, I don't like taking the pain meds & since marijuana is now legal, I received the suggestion to try that. Apparently I cannot inhale. My 70-year old husband tried teaching my 63-year old self the rudimentaries of smoking a joint. I failed abysmally but Pete was very relaxed.

GUESS THE RIGHT SIDE FELT LEFT OUT

My doctor called late this afternoon (2/11) and said the sentinel lymph nodes from my left side came back clear of cancer. However....and I said "The right breast had cancer" and he said "Yes". I KNEW IT - WHEN ARE THESE PEOPLE GOING TO LISTEN TO ME??? I didn't say that to him. Anyway, the tumor on the left side was 1.5 inches which is 3.7 cm; the one on the right is 7 times smaller at 5 millimeters. Since I no longer have a right breast, they cannot look for the sentinel lymph node on the right. He will be discussing this with other physicians to see if they have to go in to randomly find lymph nodes on the right or do ultrasounds. In either event, I will be doing Anti-hormone therapy. I am feeling frustrated as we asked about an ultrasound on the right side prior to surgery so they could have done the process to find a sentinel lymph node on that side too & we were more or less told it'd be unlikely there would be cancer on both sides but they would send both to pathology. These people obviously do not know me. Anyhow, overall good news hampered a bit by the inability to find the sentinel node on the right.

Update: In the wee hours of this morning, I have decided I will be contacting the U of M Rogel Breast Cancer Center for a second opinion on the issue with the lymph nodes on the right side. Dammit.

WELL, F A DUCK

There's a big old goose walking through our back yard but I'm still going with F_ _ _ a Duck.

I sent an email to the 'cancer person' at Sparrow expressing concern that there is no way of checking the sentinel lymph nodes on my right side. Dr McKenna just called to explain.

He said the tumor on the right side was so small that it may not have shown up yet on an ultrasound; they are not concerned with the lymph nodes on the right side. He added any future treatments would affect both sides anyway. I'm thinking "Future treatments? Whatcha talkin' about Willis....." so I said "I thought I would just need non-HRT therapy with the mastectomy". The things they don't tell you.

In discussions with the triad of physicians prior to surgery, we understood that - for me - with a double mastectomy, only non-HRT therapy would be needed. Ends up that is based on what is being seen on the ultrasound at that time. Ends up that with lobular cancer, the tumor is often larger than what is seen on the ultrasound. Ends up that the tumor on the left side was 4x larger than what was on the ultrasound. Ends up that this could be a game-changer & we have no idea what is in our near future. Based on what comes back in a test in a couple weeks, I may or may not have chemo or radiation. Hells bells, I thought I was getting off easy!!!! (Kind of sick that I consider a double mastectomy 'getting off easy'.) In any case, this sucks. Maybe not, but really???? We had no freakin' idea that what was discussed was 'in theory' only.

He is meeting with a panel of doctors on Thursday to determine if they should do an ultrasound/whatever on the right lymph nodes & will notify me of that decision. The rest is back to a waiting game.

I did call U of M for a second opinion this morning and they are getting back with me in 24-48 hours.

STILL HAVE MY PUPPY DOG BOSOM

Was hoping to get rid of the drains at yesterday's doctor appointment but Dr. McKenna wants them in until Monday or Tuesday; I made an appointment for Monday morning.

We went over the pathology report with him; it is completely unknown if the tumor in the right side was also a primary or a metastasis from the left side. The one on the right was .5 mm while the one in the right was 3.75 cm (about 1.5 "). The tumor in the left breast was actually two but they are counting them as one as they 'joined'. Dr. McKenna said since this was a slow-growing tumor, it could have been growing for 4-5 years. Glad I got those mammograms :(

There are two things we are waiting on to determine any future treatments:

-The "mammoprint" results, which indicate a chance of recurrence, will be provided on 2/25 when we see the oncologist. Since that date is exactly two months after Christmas, we are hoping this will be a good present.

-Results of lymphoscintigraphy. If you want the short story: a procedure to find the sentinel node on the right side, skip to Explanation Done. If you want the longer version, continue reading:

As you all know, since they were not expecting cancer in the right breast, they did not check the right axillary lymph nodes. Without a breast, they cannot do the procedure to find the sentinel node. Dr. McKenna met with a panel of doctors & presented the following options to check for cancer in the right lymph nodes.

-Ultrasound

-Pet scan in about a month once everything from the surgery settles down

-Sentinel node biopsy – even though the right breast is gone, it is possible to do this but with only 65 percent accuracy in finding the sentinel node. In a study of 20 malignancies, 13 were found. With 65% accuracy, this is the most - well - accurate option of the 3.

He then went on to say to increase the accuracy of a sentinel node biopsy, a lymphoscintigraphy can first be done to try to map to the sentinel node. It's basically the same procedure done prior to surgery for the left breast except dye will be inserted near the incision on the right side & the radiologist will track the movement for an hour & hopefully, this will lead to the sentinel node. If it does, the sentinel node biopsy will be done. If it does not, an ultrasound will be done followed by a pet scan in a month. The lymphoscintigraphy will be scheduled for the week of 2/18.

EXPLANATION DONE

Now you know what we know. U of M hasn't called back so I will call them today. For the rest of the day, I will do my boring schedule of waking up at an ungodly hour, taking my thyroid, giving Marley her thyroid, having cups of tea while reading the paper on my ipad, keeping up with social media, putting ice on the incisions, watching it snow, doing my arm exercises, try to do other exercises, watching it snow, nap, read a book, nap, watching it snow.....

SHOWERS AND MISC.

We'll start with the miscellaneous.

I heated up soup for my breakfast this morning & as I'm walking by Marley's dog dish, she looks up at me with sad eyes. I thought "It must be boring to be a dog & eat the same slop every day". Then I thought of our two "Steve" friends whose menu consists of 4 items....I don't know if I should give Marley a grilled cheese or give The Steve's some Purina.

When I called the U of M early Tuesday morning I was distinctly told "You will receive a call in 24-48 hours. If you don't hear from them by Thursday, call again.". I waited until Friday and was told "That 24-48 hours is after they receive all of your patient records.". The conversation ensued:

D - "Have you received all of my records?"

UM - "No"

D - "If you can tell me what you are waiting for, I will call the dr's office & remind them to send it."

UM - After an extended pause: "I don't know."

D - "It would be helpful for the initial call for the patient to be told they would be called 24-48 hours after records are received instead of 24-48 hours after the phone call."

UM - "Yes"

While I agree the U of M is a great hospital, they have issues which we discovered with my daughter's visits but that's for another day.

I had another miscellaneous topic but I have no damn idea what that was; being off hormones is not helping my mental stability.

So....Showers. My sister, Rita, asked if I ever got around to taking a shower; the answer is yes, a few of them. For as long as I can remember, prepping for a shower includes turning on the water to heat up, taking off one's clothes, adjusting the water temp, enter the shower, clean up, occasionally shave legs & underarms, dry off, exit the shower. Pretty easy. Since I'm not a nudist I also get re-dressed. Post-mastectomy includes a few extra steps:

-At least 30 minutes prior, empty drains then sit down & rest a bit.

-Be sure shampoo, conditioner, soap, shaving cream, razor etc is at a level it can be reached while seated.

-Get the dog's step stool, cover it with a towel & put it in the shower. (Remember, I don't have a shower chair so I substituted the folding stool the dog uses to get into the car; it's red with white polka dots.)

-Take off the lovely button-down Goodwill shirt of the day, first unpinning the drain bulbs & placing them on the counter. Do not step away after doing this as it is quite painful to just have the bulbs hanging (the positive of this is you only step away once).

-Take gauze covering off drains

-Have "Dexter" put Glad Press and Seal around drains being careful not to put it over the incisions (putting this on the incisions is another thing we learned you will only do once).

-Put on otherwise useless post-mastectomy camisole inside out & put drain bulbs in the pockets; do not zip it

-Preheat & adjust the water temperature

-Finish undressing

-Remove the handheld portion of the showerhead; it is important to have the 'fixed' portion also spraying water or it gets awful dang cold in there real fast, even with the camisole

-Enter the shower & sit on the dog's step stool

-Proceed slooooowwwlllly with grooming

-Turn off water

-Stand up

-Put hand-held spigot back into showerhead

-Towel dry hair & wrap that towel around camisole to keep it from dripping down one's legs. (The camisole cannot yet be re-

moved because there is no place to put the drain bulbs.) Use 2nd towel to dry lower extremeties.
-Exit the shower
-Remove camisole, put bulbs on bathroom counter. Remember to not move after this step.
-Remove Press & Seal.
-Call spousal unit in to re-apply gauze bandages
-Put on clean button-down Goodwill shirt of the day
-Pin drains to the shirt; one can now move
-Finish dressing
-Collapse into the recliner
-Return to shower to pick up toiletries so husband doesn't slip on them when he showers.

Yesterday, I thought I could take a big girl shower & just stand. Without following the complete protocol, I forgot to have Pete cover the drains with Press and Seal so it was a quick shower. Afterward, I realized I need to continue using the step stool for a bit. Stamina is not quite pre-surgery.

The adventure continues. Enjoy your day!

YOWZERS

Holy Mama my chest was on fire in the wee hours of the morning. At night, I take 2 Tylenol & a benadryl. Basically, it does nothing but let me sleep a few hours at a time. Please note I am not complaining at all as there are far worst things, just stating the facts Ma'am. The sorest part during this has been where they took the lymph nodes under my left arm. The larger part - which you would think would be worse - generally feels like a bad sunburn. Last night, it was burning lava. I'm guessing it is the skin 'adhering' to the chest underneath. But, I'm no Einstein so really don't know.

Pete & I had another first yesterday when we went in & I applied for a medical marijuana card. Who would've thunk it? You all know I was a dismal failure at inhaling so we figured we'd try the edibles. It takes 2-5 weeks to get the license, by that time it'll likely be too late to know if this helps but what the heck. It's always good to have new experiences. If anyone has sample edibles out there, let me know :)

Had some good times Friday & yesterday with neighbors, friends & family. It's great to have visitors and feel "normal". Thanks for the new memories. Late this morning we are going to my Mom's for an hour or so, then be back in time for my nap.

Oh....Dr. McKenna called me yesterday & he will be scheduling the lymphoscintigraphy (couldn't say that for $1000, I'll try it once I get the marijuana license). If that procedure shows the sentinel node on the right side, he will schedule a sentinel node biopsy (remember that's the part that hurts the worst on the left side). Also, our wonderful cousin-in-law has given us the opportunity to get a second opinion from another doctor. I am

calling him Monday; if I can get in there, we will bypass U of M.
Hey - wishes to all for a good Sunday.

SUNBURN

Apparently the burning sensation is the nerves trying to regenerate. I hope they get a move on. From what I understand, this can take 2-4 weeks. I truly am making a list of things others should know prior to a mastectomy. Yes, I would definitely do this again but it would be very helpful to have some idea of what is in store. Just when the incision starts feeling better, the skin falls apart :) I am not a believer in "What you don't know can't hurt you"; I'd rather be prepared for unpleasantness rather than blindsided by it.

And speaking of unpleasantness, my drains finally come out this morning. If for any reason, the physican changes his mind, I'm pulling them out myself. I don't mind so much walking around like a lactating dog but I am getting tired of the swelling & pain they cause at the drain 'site'. I think I might be a tad cranky this morning....

Our daughter Rebecca has the - hopefully - final excision of the melanoma today. She is such a good person; we will be grateful when this is behind her. She will have skin checks every 3 months & we pray for no further melanoma.

That's all I've got; I have to go exercise, groom, & get off my butt for the day. For those of you off work for President's Day - enjoy your holiday. (For those of us retired: every day is President's Day except the banks are usually open! Of course, we don't usually go to a bank anyways but now I'm rambling...I'm sure you're all surprised by that.)

MONDAY 2/18
UPDATE

Marley got her monthly heartworm & flea prevention this morning.

Rebecca's excision went well. She has a 4" incision & they believe they reached the 'clear margins'; this will be confirmed by a pathology report in about 2 weeks.

The drains are out!!!!! My lymphocblahblahblah is scheduled for tomorrow (2/20) afternoon. The results of this will determine if they can do a sentinel node biopsy or if one of the other options will be needed. For those of you wondering, the dye will be injected above the right scar; I will be re-slathering that area in lidocaine & plastic wrap before going to Sparrow. As painful as I now know it is, I'm hoping they can do the sentinel node biopsy as it is the most accurate.

Faxed $40 of info to the referred doctor in Flint. I talked with - gee, don't know if it was a nurse, scheduler, whatever but we decided I would fax all my pathology info for his review. If he can give an opinion based on that, great & I won't need to take up his time. Otherwise, we will set up an appointment. Thank you Ann-Margaret & Frank!!!

Pete found our missing mail on the tractor.

Little Miss Juliana should be joining Alicia, Evan, Marshall and soon Harrison tomorrow or Wednesday. Alicia & Evan are taking on quite a bit here; wishes, prayers & love to them. We will help them however we can. We jumped from 7 grandkids & 1 3/4 great-grandkids to 2 3/4 great-grandkids.

I really need to check into getting on one of those white-trash talk shows.

GOLF

I know it's shocking I'd even be thinking of golf especially since my ideal course is 6 holes with 6 adult beverages. Anyway....our dear friend Lyn Doerr used to say that male golf instructors should have to try to swing with a set of breasts hanging on their chest so they can better teach women golfers.

I'll take one for the team this summer & put this to a test. I can do one hole with prosthesis & one hole without and see which provides a better golf swing. Anticipating the question, I don't think there's a need to try a prosthesis on just one side. And, to those that have seen me golf: Bite Me, I know I'll still only hit the ball 50 yards.

REVELATION #2

I think I've got the item causing the big differences between men and women figured out - it is the beneficial effects of female hormones. Yes, I know they can make one batty at certain times of the month but nonetheless, stick with me here.

Since my hysterectomy in 2005, I've been on a small dose of hormone replacement therapy. Since my breast cancer diagnosis, I had to stop all hormones. I feel a tad unfocused some times, don't seem to do as well on multiple tasking, wanted to wash the rear camera on the car, thinking of golf, have an urge to spit....No offense guys, have patience, be kind as it appears I'm about to join your ranks.

I'M ON A ROLL TODAY

Sparrow Hospital has a breast clinic that one first attends when it is suspected you have breast cancer. The ultrasounds, mammograms, biopsies, whatever are done here. You return to see the "Breast Health Care Navigator" to receive your diagnosis. If you have cancer, she sets you up to attend the Breast Clinic for an orientation and to see the various doctors. This is all a very feel-good approach & makes one feel as if you will be taken care of very well throughout the process.

Except for my surgeon, who has been very good, they all disappear.

I just called the Herbert-Herman Cancer Center at Sparrow and asked if they have an area that answers questions after the fact & she said she didn't think so. I then called the Breast Health Care Navigator (how many hours & meetings do you think it took to come up with that title?) & asked her the same question. She said they have a follow-up meeting for patients who will be receiving radiation or chemo but not surgery. I shared that it would be nice to have a pre-mastectomy clinic to inform the patients of what could be expected post-surgery, such as your drain sites will hurt, your incisions will start to heal then your chest will burn like holy hell. OK, I didn't use those exact terms. I went on to explain this info should be shared by the hospital ahead of time so I'm not having to find answers from Facebook Groups. She told me it would be good to share this with Patient Experiences. I called Patient Experiences & they suggested I start with the Breast Health Care Navigator. I explained that is where I started. I left my name & phone # and told her I would be happy to discuss this with whomever is deemed the appropriate party because the ball is sure dropped post-orientation. "Here's your surgery date, don't let the door hit you in the backside."

In my idle time, I will be following up with them. They will develop a program just to get me off THEIR backsides.

MEETING MISS JULIANA

Here I am at 3:43 in the morning, been awake since 12:30 a.m., fixed myself a cup of Sleepytime Tea & I'm hoping it lives up to its' name.

Pete & I were leaving Sparrow late this afternoon as Alicia was walking in to pick up her sister / "foster" daughter. I asked if we could come along & meet her and we did. Juliana is now almost a month old and weighs 6+ pounds. Pete and I were able to hold her & I got to feed her. She has dark blue eyes and reddish blonde hair. The little babe has had a bit of a rough 4 weeks but is going home to a family that loves & welcomes her.

Alicia & Evan have my little sweetie Marshall and are expecting the 2nd little sweetie, Harrison, on March 20th. They have taken on the responsibility of Juliana and I have to applaud them for this; they will have a 22-month old, a 2 month old and a new baby. Juliana may currently be a temporary resident with them but she now has a place in my heart as a great-granddaughter. She's probably awake now too so she might as well have come home with me :) We pretty much have the same schedule.

I will come out & say I truly hope this little babe is never returned to her birth mother; we've been there, done that with her other six children that were finally taken away from her. Frankly, I am horrified she had another baby. There are some things in this world I do not understand; one of them is why does a drug addict get an opportunity to get clean after the baby is born? A woman pretty much knows no later than 5 weeks after conception that she is pregnant. I will generously allow six weeks. That gives her 7.5 months to stop drugs. The baby is born with drugs in its' system so after 7.5 months of choosing to harm that baby, the mom gets additional time to get clean? Excuse me!!!! I'm frustrated with this asinine thinking. I'd appreciate any insight. Keep in mind this is not the first child this mom has had with drugs in the baby's system at birth. I understand the intricacies of drug abuse & sympathize with the families going through this, that isn't the issue. The issue is allowing someone to keep a baby who was born with drugs in its' system. If a mom doesn't take care of a baby before it's born, she sure isn't going to take care of it after it's born. Being pregnant is the easy part.

That aside, I am grateful for people like Alicia & Evan that will care for this child. They have chosen to help this infant, we will assist them as much as we can, & Pete and I willingly accept this little baby as our newest great-grandchild. I hope God blesses & helps Alicia and Evan's family as they proceed with this and again I pray Juliana stays safe within a family that is drug-free and loves her.

MY PUBLIC SERVICE ANNOUNCEMENT REGARDING DENSE BREASTS

I've been getting a mammogram regularly since I was 40; regularly means every year. The last few years, the results to me & to my doctor stated the mammogram is normal with another paragraph that the breast tissue is dense. Since the mammogram said normal, I've never worried about this. MISTAKE!! If your mammogram comes back to say you have dense breasts, insist on an MRI.

As you know, I had an ultrasound & I was lucky the tumor was found as an ultrasound is not designed to look at the entire breast; typically specific quadrants are researched. The ultrasound I had indicated a relatively small tumor of 0.9 x 0.7 x. 0.5 cm. When the pathology was done post-surgery, it was 3.75 cm. Furthermore, it is believed this tumor had been growing 4-5 years; an MRI would have found it when it was miniscule. Also be aware that a "breast cancer risk" assessment may be done to determine if you should have an MRI; my risk was extremely low. Don't let the results of this determine if you should have an MRI.

Just to put it out there - if you have dense breasts & your insurance will not cover a breast MRI, the Flint Regional Medical Imaging Center does 4-D mammograms at a reduced price. Dr.

David Strahle is one of the owners of the Center & is a huge proponent of MRI's to detect breast cancer. He suggests a 4-D mammogram every two years, currently the patient cost is about $375.00 - less than a dollar a day for the two year period. Dr. Strahle indicated they have found tumors as small as 2 mm. I would strongly encourage anyone diagnosed with dense breasts to do regular MRI's.

Since I did not set a good example with my mammogram results, allow me to be your warning. :)

NO SURPRISE HERE

The lymphoscintigraphy had a 50-66% chance of finding a sentinel node. The dye just sort of sat there & did nothing. An ultrasound will be done next week.

My public service announcement on this portion is if you have breast cancer on one side, insist on an MRI on the other side. They will tell you it's not needed because any cancer will be found post-surgery in the pathology report. The problem is after surgery, they cannot find the sentinel node.

Why must I continually be a lesson to others???? And, you are welcome.

BIOFREEZE - COOL THE PAIN

Horsehockey. That crap burns!!! Thank God I'm finally taking big-girl stand-up showers cuz I sure needed one in a rush last evening. We had to pick up a prescription at Meijer so I asked Pete if we could go inside so I could find something to calm down these overly-heated chest & underarm areas.

I previously tried Benadryl Itch Cooling Spray, which we already had at home. This does a fair job but I don't like the residual stickiness which causes my arms to be stuck to my sides. Also at home was Panama Jack Green Ice, works about the same as the Benadryl Spray with the same stickiness. I perused the aisles at Meijers for a spray, not a cream cuz putting on a cream would be far too painful. I first saw a spray stating "calms the burning itch" but it was Jock Itch spray. While I may be turning into a man, I have yet to develop testicles. I then spied Biofreeze "Cool the Pain" Spray & purchased that.

First of all, this stuff sprays all over the damn place. I thought I was aiming toward my chest but it ended up in my mouth & on my neck; I do not recommend ingesting this. I finally got it onto the correct areas & at first, sure it cooled things down. For about 3 minutes then it turned into fire. I'm like WTH. I tried wiping it off with one of Marshall's diaper wipes & that seemed to intensify it. So I sped into the shower & was able to get most of it off. I also changed my shirt so the spray that got on the shirt wasn't reapplied to my skin. I do not recall signing up to do product reviews but that apparently is another side-effect of a mastectomy that no one told me about.

Speak of untold side effects, a representative from Sparrow called me yesterday stating she was from the 7th floor Surgical area & was told I had some concerns I wanted to share. I told her they did a great job, my concern was with the breast clinic; that is where I started this issue & that's where it belongs. Passing the buck seems to be a popular past time at that facility.

And speaking of bucks - well, actually squirrels, I hear my husband pumping his pellet gun. He's been trying to shoot a squirrel off the bird feeder for a couple days. I truly hope I don't have to call our friends Ruby & Galen to get their Squirrel Gumbo recipe. If he also kills the possum that's been around, we could have a real feast. Geesh, he just came into the office to get a rifle. Guess the squirrel had on a pellet-proof vest. Guess I better give Ruby a call for that recipe.

One other thing of note & this is definitely kicking you while you're down. I know I mentioned I joined a Facebook group for double mastectomy patients. I've actually gleaned some useful information from it. Our Facebook page says Diann-Pete; Pete reads it but I don't recall him ever updating it. The group administrator of the double mastectomy page sent me a message yesterday that they are booting me off that page because "it is only for women". Men get breast cancer too. A big 'bite me' to them. I'm thinking of rejoining with a name like Sidney, Pat, Corrie, Fran...

Well, gotta go, the washer just finished a cycle. The thought is currently running through my mind that I should have washed that shirt by itself first rather than with the rest of the laundry. I'm hoping the biofreeze washed off rather than spread to the other clothes. I'll put a pair of Pete's boxers on the top of his stack & will keep ya posted. :)

A WHOLE LOT OF NOTHING...

I'm starting to go stir crazy; it is recommended to walk after surgery to build up one's stamina. The jackass that suggests that obviously does not live in Michigan during the Winter. I have been using my step thing in the basement in 20 minute increments. I want to get out but after about 60 minutes, it's time to rest.

So, doctors and their percentages & risks.....bite me. My family doctor, who is wonderful, did a Gail Breast Cancer Risk Calculation prior to sending me for my original ultrasound. This Calculator was developed by the National Cancer Institute; if you want to know more, google it. :) My 5-year risk for cancer is 1.3%, lifetime risk is 5.7%. And yet, I had cancer in both breasts. No need to reiterate the issue with the right sentinel lymph node but 3 doctors have said "Don't worry, there's only a 3-5% chance you would have cancer in that node.". Yea, well I had a 1.3% chance of developing cancer in the next 5 years & look at that! What is the percentage of 3 family members being diagnosed with cancer within one month? What is the percentage of winning the Lotto? I better buy a ticket.

Excuse me a bit while I respond to some FB messages; we are picking up 2 baby swings today; one for Juliana, one for Harrison. I'm going to have to look for bunkbed pack-and-plays. I am no longer giving away any baby items; every time I do, a new infant pops up.

Another item noticed today - oh crap, the washer is dinging

again - be right back. A woman's work is never done! Speak of which, the housecleaners I hired suck. Their lists state "clean the interior windows", I have to find out what that entails cuz they sure didn't wash them. The owner is smart though, she stopped in & left a large bouquet of flowers. The flowers are pretty but also make me feel hesitant to complain. I'll get over it.

Oh - back to "another item noticed today". Good heavens, my mind wanders. You all know Pete & I got kicked off the double mastectomy FB page. There are others "Flat & Fabulous", "Fantastic Flat Fashions" etc etc. What they should be is "Concave & Cute" "Hollow & Hot" etc. The swelling in my chest is going down leaving 2 empty 'bowls'. Another unknown item but I cannot complain as they will be handy for holding popcorn, ice cream (while soothing the burn at the same time), nuts, etc. If I forget to take my earrings out at night, it will be a handy place to store them till I get up the next time. To my current knowledge, no one has shared this "benefit". If the bastards hadn't kicked us off the page, I could ask about this. I know, start a new FB account just for these groups; I plan to but just not yet. I'm pouting & I'm entitled to do that. I've been very steady during this entire crappy 2 months but one of these days, I'm having a hissy fit. I know this could all be worse but all the same.....

That's it for now, talk with ya soon. PS - Squirrel Update: Pete has only shot one of twenty so no gumbo for now. And we were so looking to seeing their little heads pop to the top of the pan.

FINALLY, SOME GREAT NEWS

Rebecca's pathology report came back this morning & they removed all of the melanoma!!!! Thanks to all (alive & in heaven) for your prayers & support. Who would think one would be grateful that she's back to dealing with "only" lupus & neuropathy? We are very relieved & eternally thankful.

I didn't write much this weekend; I've been resting. We met Becky's family for an hour on Saturday morning for breakfast, then Brad, Tricia, Ava, Lexi & Marshall stopped by, we then went to pick up a few groceries at Meijer. Oh - we also stopped at the video store & picked up a couple infant swings. Meijer was our last stop & I ended up sitting at the "old people's bench" waiting for Pete to check out. Guess I should have saved the video store & getting the swings for another day. How am I going to know my limits if I don't occasionally exceed them? Yes, I realize they should be extended little-by-little not by a lot.

That said, however, today we have medical appointments at 11:00, 2:40, and 7:00. 11:00 is with my back doctor to discuss why the relatively painful rhizotomies are not working; 2:40 is with the oncologist to get the results of the mammoprint & to discuss Wednesday's ultrasound; 7:00 - doesn't matter, I'm hoping to be in a drug-induced sleep as I'm having another MRI on my back. Ain't no way I'm going in that tube fully conscious. Looking at my day today, I guess there's a reason I was sitting on that old people's bench - sounds like I'm joining their ranks temporarily. And then, honey, the doctor said....

My doctor did give me something to help me sleep; it didn't work. Still woke up every 3 hours. I bought OTC Unisom and actually the last 2 nights, I'd wake up but actually go back to sleep. I may have found a new favorite drug. I'll try tonight "Unisom-less" to see how it goes. Of course, I'll still have the drug in my system from the MRI so should sleep soundly. I was going to say "like a baby" but then I'd be up every few hours. I wonder what ninny coined that term. Obviously a childless hermit. I'll schedule Tuesday night to try without Unisom.

I will let you know the results of the appointment with the Oncologist - Christmas was exactly 2 months ago (I know, it seems longer) and we already got a wonderful Christmas gift with Rebecca's news this morning so we are expecting another this afternoon. Maybe I'll walk in with a huge bow on my head; if nothing else, it'll convince the dr I am nuts.

MAMMOPRINT

This test showed a low risk of breast cancer recurrence so chemo is not needed. I start pills tomorrow to block hormones produced by my body; these will be taken for five years. Although I've been getting bone density tests for 20 years, they want another as a baseline; I will need blood drawn every month to check liver enzymes (both are for tracking any effects of the pills). I see the oncologist again in 3 months. Now if we could just find those pesky right auxiliary lymph nodes.....

BTW - it really hurts to close one's finger in the dishwasher.

MRI

Another sadist developed these things & that person put his/her sister at the front window as the receptionist. Just an unrelated point of interest: it is quite painful using my index finger to type - well, nowadays it is called keyboarding - that dishwasher did a number on my poor digit.

When an MRI is scheduled, the patient is asked if they are claustrophobic and if the answer is yes, they are advised to get a relaxant prior to the MRI. In the past, I have used valium to quite a good degree of success. This time my doctor gave me 1 Atavan; when I found out this particular MRI would be 2 hours, she gave me another. The first 1 mg Atavan did nothing. I took the second, still nothing. Panic is seeping throughout my body. We approach the window at the MRI area and the sadist's cruelest sister says "They show you in M1, are you claustrophobic?". I replied "YES"; her reply? "Oh, they should have put you in M3 which is much larger". She goes on to explain it's much more comfortable, too bad I'm not in there & I finally said "OK, it's best not to discuss this any further". I clearly deduced the only reason the scheduler asks if you are claustrophobic is so if the answer is yes, they put you in the smallest tube they have. Panic is now settling into my soul.

The appointment is running 30 minutes late & I'm thinking "crap the little bit of effect this stuff is having is going to run out before I even get in there". At the 40-minute late mark, the MRI runner person comes to get me. If you haven't had an MRI, you put on a blue hospital shirt & pants (you can pretend to be a doctor), put on their little slippers, remove anything & everything that is metal then you are placed on a 3" wide table to be shoved into a 12" wide tube - head first. Oh, and your head is placed between 2 padded blocks so it cannot move; just like if you were going for a lobotomy - just be forewarned. Back to the size of the MRI itself: imagine stacking Cheerios or Fruit Loops in a line then trying to insert a drinking straw through those tiny holes. If you are cheap, imagine using Great Value O's or Froot Rings. The result is the same. (For the stringent ecologists out there, yes I know plastic straws shouldn't be used anymore; paper or metal can be substituted, no fair using 'cocktail' straws.)

Since my back is sore, the radiologist kindly put pillows under my knees. I thought "that's nice of her"....until I felt my knees hit the 'roof' of the MRI the same time my elbow hit the side. You all know what I was thinking so no need to write it. I pulled my arms in & crossed them over my body while retaining a firm grip on the 'panic button' one is given. I'm then thinking oh hell, I'm positioned just like a mummy. The radiologist says "think good thoughts"; yea, well those good thoughts included lining up members of the various medical equipment development teams over stumps like a bunch of turkeys at Thanksgiving. And I was running the guillotine.

I tried deep-breathing which reminded me if I move 1/100th of an inch, I'd be touching the walls of this machine. I tried picturing the faces of my grandbabies which reminded me that I'd probably never survive this to see them again. I tried thinking of beautiful places we visited which just reminded me of the fact that is where I was supposed to be now instead of stuffed inside a piece of ziti pasta. I know the medication was working somewhat or I would have been scrambling like a crab out of that thing. It worked enough to keep me from going into full-blown panic.

On our way home, I told Pete I am having a big glass of honey whiskey when we get home. I poured some, drank a sip & went right to sleep. Should have taken a shot of that to the hospital!

The results of the MRI should be back in a couple days. The ultrasound on my axillary nodes is Wednesday; I'm just one big medical guinea-pig.

GOTTA BE HUMAN

I can make jokes, I can be happy, I can get along but there are times when this is not easy. I'm frustrated with making plans to see those we enjoy then being too damn tired to follow through with them. I'm sick of medical professionals who don't listen thus making things 1000 times more difficult. I am sick of freaking winter, I am sick of my chest & arms hurting, I am frustrated with not being given the 'whole' picture, being told only what some "expert" feels is "appropriate". I'm frustrated with following up with doctor's offices because things don't get scheduled as promised. I'm tired of the people in this world who lie or blame everyone but themselves for their mistakes and of those who hear one side of a story & then actively choose to cause pain for the other side. I am tired of being worn out after exercising for 15-20 minutes. I'm tired of not being able to cover up with a sheet or blankets because the touch of them hurts. I'm sick of medical tests that tell me nothing. I've had enough of sleeping between pillows rather than next to Pete. I'm tired of when asked how I am & I reply that I'm fine being requestioned (that ain't even a word or a grammatically correct sentence). I'm tired of movies with stupid endings; I'm sick of books that are drivel, I'm through with wiping the snow off the dog's paws. All that said, I know I'm lucky; this life could be a million times worse. Thanks to those in our lives that care for your love, friendship & support. Right now I'm climbing into my bed with its' electric blanket & pouting a little.

Cripes, I don't know how guys cross their arms across their damned chests, without boobs, my arms now slide up too high. I think we all need to pay attention to this - betcha women tend more to cross their arms across their upper abdomen while men's are across their upper chest.

RIGHT SIDE ULTRA SOUND

We went back to Sparrow today for an ultra sound of the right auxiliary lymph nodes & a possible biopsy. I get called in, go into the room, take my coat off & the ultra sound tech is chatting & asked if I'd had surgery yet. I politely replied, yes on February 4th but wanted to yell "I'm flatter than most men - what do you think?". She did the ultrasound, got the doctor, the doctor redid the ultrasound and said (good heavens, that phrase sounds like "..no more monkeys jumping on the bed") based on how things haven't exactly gone as they expected so far, she could biopsy a node that looked a tad different from the rest. So, that's what was done. Results should be available in a couple days. No, I have not heard anything on Monday night's MRI for my back.

Back to lymph nodes - the thing with these nodes is even if the sentinel one is clear, cancer could have spread to others. It's good to test the sentinel node but is not a guarantee at all. Sparrow really needs better education for their patients.

The doctor was very informative; she said it is difficult to find lobular cancer with a 'fatty breast' and with dense ones, like mine *were*, it is nearly impossible. Tumors show up white on a mammogram & an ultrasound; if one's breast are the 'good' kind and are fatty (who'd think that was ever good), the breast tissue shows up dark & the tumors are easily seen. With dense breasts, the breast tissue appears white so tumors are not readily found. I was advised to continue to pursue getting a 2nd opinion with U of M. No, they aren't going to say stitch those babies back on;

that was still a wise thing to do. They just may have other opinions on treatment. I'm fortunate I had the ultra sound tech I did on the first ultrasound as this person said based on looking at the ultra sound results, she would have said 'don't worry about it, come back in 6 months'. The doctor explained to her that lobular cancer often looks small in the ultrasound but is much larger in reality. So, I dodged that one bullet. We also discussed doing a Pet scan in about 4 months after everything from the mastectomy has settled down.

We got home around 4:30, I went to bed & slept till 6:00 then we watched Marshall & Juliana for a couple hours while Evan and Alicia had their maternity tour at Sparrow. Marshall is a sweetheart; he's learning to talk and is just a funny toddler. Juliana was very good; she didn't even fuss during her bath. And now I've been up 4.5 hours so it's probably time to go back to bed.

WORDS OF THE DAY

No, these are nothing insightful, just words off the results of my back MRI. "Severe bone marrow edema, levoscoliosis, severe degenerative disk disease". Doesn't that all sound great?

My primary physician and my back doctor both called yesterday afternoon requesting that I have blood work done to detect infection which could cause the edema. Of course, these came back normal. I never thought I'd be frustrated with receiving "normal" test results. Where do we go from here? No idea. Apparently when one has breast cancer, the rest of the body goes to pot too. Speak of pot - still haven't got that medical marijuana license.

I have an appointment with my back doctor next Friday 3/8 to discuss the MRI results. I've asked my primary physician for a referral to the U of M Back & Pain Center for a second opinion. I might as well move to Ann Arbor.

Took a shower this morning, thought about just spending the whole day in there.......

WHAT I LEARNED YESTERDAY

Tacos in the crockpot can be made without first browning the hamburg.

The lymph node they removed on Wednesday is ok.

Alicia hopes to deliver Harrison before most of her family are in Florida for a week. He is due March 20th, Pete & I leave on the 19th, the rest on the 22nd.

After babysitting Marshall, I need a nap. These days though, I need a nap after watching paint dry.

Vitamin E oil probably does nothing for scarring, but I'm trying it anyways.

HELLO

Well, how has everyone been? I've not updated this in a few days. As most of you know from Facebook, we went to the P-W State Finals Cheer Competition on Saturday (our granddaughter Ella is on the team); they took 1st place which was an amazing accomplishment. Ava & Lexi came home with us to spend the night. Apparently Ava and Lexi were revisiting their early childhood as they were playing the board games we used to play together when they were 2-4 years old.

The Cheer Competition was at the Deltaplex in Grand Rapids; tickets are purchased in advance, seats are assigned & the seats are squished together - sideways and legways (not a word but you know what I mean). After an hour of just waiting to get my chest poked, I went down to the female security guard, told her I'd recently had a mastectomy and I was nervous sitting like sardines and asked if I could sit in the handicapped area, which was empty. She graciously said yes so I enjoyed sitting all by myself watching the girls. Well, not all by myself as two workers came & sat nearby & as my son-in-law says "You will talk to anyone." so we chatted throughout the competition.

Anyways....Ava & Lexi were here Sunday; Brad & Tricia picked them up mid-afternoon. Always enjoy having the grandkids. Monday (yesterday), I met 3 friends for lunch then came home and slept for 2.5 hours. Guess I had to make up for no naps on Saturday & Sunday.

Still having trouble sleeping through the night despite trying a prescription and then Unisom (not together). An acquaintance gave me two "pot brownies" so I decided to try one last night. It didn't taste horrible, some thoughtful baker had put mini chocolate chips in them. I slept pretty darned good but when I got up to use the bathroom, I walked in there, stopped, & thought "What the hell am I doing in here?". Next time, I will try 1/2 a brownie. I will never be a drug addict.

For the rest of this week, I have a bone density test tomorrow & an appointment with the back doctor Friday morning. Boy, do I feel like a senior citizen: naps, doctor appointments, no idea why I went into the bathroom......

Enjoy this snowy day.

A SUCCESS!

Maybe putting that in large letters is a tad of an overstatement. It was a success, a small success, a semi-success, not a dismal failure....I was able to lay on my right side for about 25 minutes last night!!!!

YAY! First time in thirty-three nights! Yes, it was only 25 minutes before I had to return to laying on my back within my fortress but still 25 minutes! Let me invite you to my nocturnal thoughts....beware, it is scary in there.

So, as I stated, I was able to lay on my right side for 25 minutes last night. I had to rest my left arm either behind me laying on Pete or across me laying on a pillow as it is still quite uncomfortable just resting an arm flat against my body. My nocturnal thoughts....I've returned to my back & just letting my mind roam and thinking 25 minutes isn't much but it takes only 10 seconds to launch a space ship. Yea - 10 seconds. The countdown starts at 10 then they say blast-off while pushing the button. Then I think well, never mind all the people who make the screws, the people that put the leather on the seats...mmm, the PETA people won't like that leather reference but suck it up buttercups, the engineers, the IT staff, the mechanics, the person that actually makes the button they push, it's still 10 seconds. If it takes only 10 seconds to launch a space ship, 25 minutes on my left side is A SUCCESS.

Here's to a happy day.

FUNNY STUFF AND INCOMPETENCE

Kindly note that is incompetence, not incontinence. There is quite a difference.

I had my bone density scan on Wednesday at the Sparrow Professional Building near Frandor. The first floor needs some clarification as a lot of people coming into the building struggle to determine where they need to go; fortunately a lot of the women have to 'go' and make their first stop the restroom.

The male & female restroom doors face the seating area for xrays & bloodwork so as one is waiting, one can see the bathroom doors. The men's room door seems to work fine; the women's room door only works with the handicap function so the door doesn't close for a very long time. The restroom is one room, no stall, with the toilet facing the door so it's important that the door closes prior to a person proceeding with their business. While I do not have an issue with incontinence, I can pee on command so after checking in, went to use the bathroom (at this point I had no knowledge of the dysfunctional door). The door opens and doesn't close then doesn't close, on and on. I tried pushing it shut but it pushes back harder. So all you can do is stand their trying not to wet your pants during the interminable time that door takes to close. After leaving the restroom, I chose to take a seat facing it. What fun! It was hilarious watching people try to close that dang door; one woman caught my eye & I smiled and waved at her. She ended up coming to sit next to me & by the time I was called in for my scan, there were four of us sitting there watching these restroom victims. If you ever have some spare time & you don't know what to do, I highly suggest going to the Sparrow Professional Building, 1st floor, and take a seat facing the restrooms. You will not be disappointed.

The U of M called yesterday & set up an appointment for their breast cancer clinic for Monday. Today, they called & said they can probably review my case without me being there on Monday. This is simply to review the plan Sparrow has laid out for me & to talk with their oncologist who will perhaps give more information on how to check for future cancer other than "I'll take care of that". And that comment leads right into incompetence.

This experience has reaffirmed something I've known a long time: If you want something done, either choose someone you know will get the job done, do it yourself, or resign yourself to hounding someone until they do what they were supposed to have done. Most of the people we've encountered through this process do not fall into the category of "....will get the job done...". The doctor who didn't think it was necessary to check the right breast for cancer, the person who is supposed to schedule your various tests and doesn't do it so you finally call the hospital yourself to schedule, the nurse that forgets to call in a prescription, the person who failed to request the blood draw you went to get, the medical marijuana company that doesn't send the id's they copied to the State, another person who didn't finalize a prescription, the person who said I could pick up a baby swing from her front porch & put the money under the door mat then there's no swing on the porch but the door mat sure is there. It can all get overwhelming & very, very frustrating.

Speaking of frustrating: I had the appointment with my back doctor this morning & I have to see a neurosurgeon. Go freakin' figure, right? My back has deteriorated a huge amount in one year; currently no explanation for that. The neurosurgeon's office is supposed to call me for an appointment (see above paragraph). I believe I already stated in an earlier post that my family doctor is referring me to the U of M Pain & Back Clinic. I confirmed with my family doctor's office this morning that this referral has been done.

On the bright side, Pete & I went to The Front Room today & picked up my prosthetic boobs & the accompanying pocket brassieres (they don't go in your pocket dumb ass, they have a pocket in which to place the prosthesis). I'm still a tad too sore to actually utilize them yet but we can take turns holding the fake boobs. Almost as much fun as watching the restroom at the Sparrow Professional Building. If we did that AND held the boobs.....

MIMI

I have referenced my mother's dog Mimi in a prior post. The thing weighs about 3 pounds & poops twice its' own weight in little chocolate chip sized doggy doo.

Now that I've ruined chocolate chip cookies for you.....why, you ask, am I writing about Mimi? Allow me to share.

Like a bad penny, some people just keep showing up in your life. One of those is our ex-daughter-in-law; the miscreant who after 12 years of our repeated efforts, finally got all 6 of her kids taken away. You know she recently had a 7th. I won't reiterate my thoughts on that and yes, this is related to Mimi. Patience, people, patience.

Years ago, Angie went to school for dog grooming & continues to occasionally groom a dog; typically when she needs drug money. Through the years, my Mom has continued to have Angie groom Mimi. I've talked with Mom about this & shared my concerns that while she thinks she's helping Angie, this is just giving her drug money. Well, after Baby #7 & Angie's horrid attitude, I told Mom I don't ask her for much but would she PLEASE stop having Angie groom her dog. I said I would find a place to have Mimi groomed, pick up Mom & Mimi, take Mimi to the groomers, Mom & I would have lunch then we'd go home. You likely think "she forgot the step of picking up the dog.". No, I did not forget....

Mom finally agreed to a new groomer saying Mimi needed a haircut within a couple weeks so I proceeded with finding a dog groomer. Who knew this could be so difficult??? Every place within the tri-county area was booked for weeks. Grrrr. I finally found a place that could do it on Monday, 3/11, let Mom know

& it's all set. Well, then the U of M called me to come to their breast clinic on 3/11 and at first I asked if we could come the following week then I came to my senses and realized I was passing this up for a DOG?? I scheduled with the U of M, called to change Mimi's appointment and there is nothing for weeks. I'm like "Good Lord, finally get Mom away from stinkin' Angie & this is becoming a huge mess.". I finally found a place that could do it today (Friday, 3/8). I called Mom & rescheduled everything then this morning while we are at the back doctor getting that good news, the groomer calls & says she's sick, can we reschedule? Excuse me but - F me!!! So, we rescheduled for Wednesday, I called Mom AGAIN , got this changed AGAIN & I know she is thinking "If I'd stayed with Angie....". An hour later U of M called to say I really didn't need to be there Monday. Reread the end of the "Excuse me" phrase.

So, Mimi is now scheduled for Wednesday which is typically my Mom's day of being at my brother & sister-in-law's ceramic shop but she sighingly said she could do that Tuesday. I've already made grooming appointments for her (Mimi, not Mom) for April & June; they said when we arrive in April, make the appointment for August. This is a hotter commodity than anything I can think of; forget being a physician, encourage your children to go to dog grooming school!

We will see what Wednesday brings; if they don't groom that mutt perfectly, my worries about my back & cancer are over as I'm sure my mother will take me out of this world.

Have a good weekend All!

JUST A BORING UPDATE

This has been a busy Sunday. The dog woke me up around 8:00 - really 7:00, stupid time change - because she needed water. Since a bomb going off in the room wouldn't wake my beloved spouse, I got up & took care of the dog. Pete left around 12:30 to attend a golf show; can't fathom why he didn't invite me :) I went back to bed & slept a couple hours, got up & tried to read, slept another hour. Watched TV, read a bit & slept again. It's 5:00 now & I don't know if I'm foggy because I need to sleep again or because I've slept too much.

The doctor from the U of M called me Friday night. We discussed options for checking the right lymph nodes & the only option sucks. She said that option - removing all the lymph nodes - is the "text book" approach but is also about 20 years old. She said since the cancer on the left was Stage 2 and the lymph nodes weren't affected, she would expect the same to be true of the right especially since that tumor was so much smaller. I said "Stage 2?? I've been told all along it was Stage 1." She replied, no, the tumor was greater than 3 cm which automatically puts it up a stage; I'm simply thrilled my tumor was such a go-getter. She was very informative & very kind to talk with; she indicated there wasn't a need for me to be there on Monday but she understands being personally there can be very 'healing' for some. We chose that we would stay home, she'd present the case, and call me Monday night. Unless one of the cancer panel members feels very strongly about choosing the 20-year old method, it would appear I can just move on with this and, I guess, focus on my back & the other myriad items. Items? you ask. My bone density scan results came back Saturday morning; looks like I'll be starting meds for osteoporosis. I have to call my doctor on Monday.

Friends were over last night & the discussion got around to the prosthesis; there were questions, so I brought one out for show and tell. Don't feel left out, if you want so see them, I'll let you. Maybe I'll just start leaving one out on the coffee table for a little conversation piece.

Wishes for a good week.

JUST WAITING

Waiting to hear from U of M regarding Monday's conference, from Lansing Neurosurgery, from U of M Neurosurgery. Giving them all one more day & I'll start making phone calls tomorrow (3/14). Our eldest granddaughter asked why I'm being sent to a brain doctor for my back; I explained neurosurgery goes beyond just the brain. Now the song from the Wizard of Oz "If I Only Had a Brain" is running through my head.

Today's the day I take Mimi to get groomed - let's hope this works out well or I'm in deep doo-doo. Marley goes in this morning to have her thyroid rechecked; we forgot the appointment 2 weeks ago. I'll pick Marley up after Mimi's appointment. Mom doesn't know it yet but she'll be riding back to her house with Marley in the car; some things are best left to the last minute.

Alicia & Evan are doing good with Marshall & Juliana; Harrison is due next week. We are hoping he enters this world before we leave on the 19th. Alicia has to take Juliana for twice weekly visits with Angie; I simply cannot bring myself to say "with her mother" as Angie - except for the swearing version - is not in any sense of the term a "mother". We watched Marshall yesterday during this 'visit'; he is an absolutely delight! He will be 2 in May & I just love this age; things are new, he's learning something every day, he is a joy to be around.

Where are we going on the 19th? We are flying to Florida a few days in advance of the Spring Break trip with the kids & the majority of the grandkids. We fly into Tampa on Tuesday, meet the families in Destin the 23rd-30th then we fly back home the following Tuesday. We are both ready to see something other than snow and/or mud.

I'm toying with the idea of breaking out the prosthesis today. I feel sort of silly wearing them around people who have already seen me flat as a pancake; well flatter than a pancake, remember the concave issue. We'll see.

Enjoy your day.

HERE'S AN UPDATE FOR YOU....

Prior to leaving home I decided it was time to try the prosthesis. OK - when you try these on at the store, they provide a t-shirt to put on over them. Here's a hint for you future cancer patients: bring your own damned shirt.

At home today, I first put these things in the camisole, which is the most comfortable option. I put on my shirt & thought - what the hell, where are the boobs? Seriously - zip, zilch, zero. So I thought maybe try the more comfortable of the 2 brassieres, still nothing. I went out to show my overly honest husband & asked - can you tell I have them in? He's like, "ummmmm sure". The dumb ass - we've been together for 20 years & he thinks I don't know when he's not truthful. I said "really?". "Ummmmm, no". I called the 'Breast Store' and they said they could upgrade free of charge. I left in the non-boobs and picked up my Mom & her rodent dog.

Mom, Mimi the rodent, & I arrive at the groomer; go over a bunch of crap & they are finally ready to take Mimi so I clarified that Mom & I would be going to lunch for an hour or so then be back to pick up the mutt. The groomer looks at me like I'm from another country (probably looking at my non-boobs) & said it takes 3-4 hours to groom a dog. WTF - that critter doesn't even weigh 4 pounds!!!! Run her through a - I don't know what - but run her through it & be done in an hour. I'm behind Mom & making motions at the groomer that my life is completely over if this damn dog is there 3-4 hours. The groomer said she can probably get her done in 2 - 2.5 hours.

Mom & I go to lunch & she doesn't even remotely notice I have boobs which confirmed I definitely needed to go up to something beyond mosquito bites. We proceed with lunch, I pull out the prosthesis - oh for heaven's sakes calm down, I did that in the bathroom, put them in my coat pockets, get to the car, restock them in the proper packaging & we go to the Breast Store. Mom waited in the car & I did a quick switch up one size. When I got back in the car, Mom confirmed she could actually tell there were bosom - real or otherwise - under my shirt. Per Mom's request, we stopped at Kohls to peruse the jewelry counter. We go to pick up Marley, check on Mimi & she has another 1/2 hour. We take Marley home, Mom comes in, leaves her shirts - ha - sorry, shoes - in a major pathway & I trip over them. Thanks Mom. We go back to get Mimi; her hair is a tad short but she had a lot of gnarly hair that needed to be cut out & thankfully the groomer chopped off that awful fu-manchu mustache she has been sporting for years. Mimi's fu-manchu not Mom's; that's another story. Yes, I can be a bitch. Mom doesn't have a mustache of any kind - really.

Mom is asking if all groomers take 4 hours so I called the salon in St. Johns which is Mimi's appointment in 6 weeks & was told that they take 1 - 1.5 hours. Since this is right next to a saloon, I believe this is doable. I get Mom & Mimi home & settled and go visit Jordan & one of her siblings. Jordan just finished the 2nd chemo treatment & opted not to have an adult beverage but Jordan's sister & I chose to imbibe. Jordan has 2 more treatments then 6 weeks of radiation. Pete & I admire & love Jordan very much (we are relatively fond of Jordan's siblings & their families too). We will all get through this.

BTW, I do have an appointment for my back with Lansing Neurology on Monday morning. And....Mom gave me some of what I thought was holy water a few weeks ago. I decided tonight that I might as well use it. It is oil, not water & I smell like bad french fries.

Pete, Marley, I & the neighbors within a mile will be dreaming tonight of being in a noxious landfill; sweet dreams to the rest of you.

ANOTHER NEW TERM

We'll start where we sort of left off with Mimi. The new term I learned on Wednesday probably applies to all dogs, not just Mimi. The groomer was checking her out & said they'd groom her "potty spot". Huh? That's a new one. Much like the term "navigator" discussed a while back, I wonder how many meetings & hours it took to come up with that ridiculous term.

I had Marshall Thursday afternoon; poor kid was thoroughly confused. I had tried to fill a prescription & was told not till 3/21. I explained we were leaving for vacation 3/19 & would need more before then. I had to call our provider & some of the questions required a reply of "no". I'd say "no", Marshall would look at me like 'what am I doing wrong?". At about the 3rd 'no', that look became 'what I am doing wrong you weirdo?". Marshall was later pointing at the TV saying 'bubble'; I finally figured out he wanted Bubble Guppies on. Good Heavens, I would be brain dead within a week if I had to watch this crap every day. I do have to admit it's funny to watch Marshall sit in a chair singing "bubble bubble bubble".

The U of M finally returned my call on Wednesday regarding my breast cancer consult. The doctor recommends another ultrasound of the right axillalry nodes in 6 months then annually for a while. She said my oncologist could order this & just send the U of M the report. I told her I was looking for a new oncologist so we decided she'd refer me to one at the U of M. I can easily make the trek to Ann Arbor every 6 months to a year.

Also on Wednesday, I had my appointment with the dermatologist for my itchy neck. She's prescribing something I need to mix with a lotion and use twice a day for 3 weeks. She told me to stop using my anti-aging creams; what I heard was "You old bat, your neck skin is thinning out & is now irritated by those products.". Before I left for that appointment, I put a note in the car to remember to pick up my 'swim boobs' on the way home. About 1/3 of the way home, I saw the note so turned around & picked those up. Guess I'm now ready for Florida. Guess I need to add those to the list of things I pack for vacations. Never thought "swim boobs" would be on my vacation list. Betcha you didn't know there was such a thing as "swim boobs". Apparently the silicone prosthesis can be quite uncomfortable when it's hot. These things have a fabric covering with some sort of beads inside; the water flows through them.

Based on the last 3 of 4 years, I was unsuccessful talking Pete into going anywhere other than Florida next year (if anything goes wrong next year, it IS his fault). I also was unsuccessful in trying to book our 'regular' place in Anna Maria & that, along with many other properties, is already full in February. I was successful in booking a couple others & in banging my head on the fireplace mantle while dusting whatever that slab of granite in front of it is called. Pete, being always sympathetic, said "I bet that hurt.".

Hoping P-W boys' basketball wins the State Championship today! Ella will be cheering so we'll be watching it on TV.

Enjoy your day.

PROSTHESIS DEBUT - DAY 2

Frankly, these things are a pain in the ass. Yes, I know that's not where they belong.

My daughter & I spent some time together on Friday. Since I only have the 1 camisole & it was in the wash, I decided to try one of the bras. Uncomfortable!! I'd read on some of the 'Flat & Fabulous' posts that Jockey makes a sports-type bra with pockets that work well. On my way to Becky's, I stopped at the Jockey outlet (bras, underwear, etc not the little guy on the horse) & tried some on. First of all, these need to be purchased 3 sizes bigger than one would wear or you will never get it over your head. That said, I tried the prosthesis in them & thought it would work. I bought 4 of them, all in different colors.

I arrived at Becky's house & brought one in to change into to get rid of the noxious garment I was wearing. When I took my coat off, she said "Oh, look, your boobs grew back!". I then went in to switch brassieres. We took off to go shopping & it quickly became obvious the fabric of the Jockey bras was far too flexible to support the light weight of the prosthesis as they were not only sliding under my arms but also working their way to my stomach. I told my daughter "Good God, if you see these all the way under my arms or on the floor, let me know.". I returned the other 3 bras.

When the boys got home from school, I could not keep myself from using Becky's terminology that my boobs grew back. They were appropriately grossed out; of course Gavin, our little strategist, replied "So'd your cancer come back too?". A snarl of the lip to him. The majority of our family will be together the week of 3/23 during spring break; five of the grandkids will be there. I told Noah & Gavin the 5 of them could all put in money & guess if I'd be wearing the prosthesis or not that day & whoever guessed correctly the most would get the money at the end of the week. They both replied they weren't going to even look at me. I should bring along the ridiculous 'knitted knockers' and hide them in strategic places during the week.....

A BEAUTIFUL NEW FAMILY MEMBER

NO, we didn't get a puppy!

Alicia & Evan's 2nd son was born this morning on St. Patrick's Day. His name is Harrison Patrick (already chosen prior to day of birth), weighed 7 lb 10 oz, lots of dark hair & he is, of course, wonderful. He simply loves his Great-Grammy :) They will have 3 kids under 2 years old; may God bless them & give them strength.

Alicia & Evan are watching Marley while we are in Florida; we leave Tuesday. I asked if this wasn't a tad much, Alicia replied "She just lays there like a rug". That is a very accurate description of our dog. Up until the last week, that was also an accurate description of me.

Our week starts off tomorrow with a visit to the neurologist for my back then transporting Marshall & Juliana to Howell as they are spending a few days with their Great-Aunt Rebecca & her family. I've been told Juliana is not happy in her car seat & will cry most of the time she is in the car. Looking real forward to that trip!

Then Tuesday we should be on our way to Florida for two weeks. Anything to do with Florida causes butterflies in my stomach at this point....hopefully this will all go smooth.

Hope ya'all have a good week.

DRIVING WHILE CRYING

Not me crying, but I was ready to beat my head against the steering wheel.

As you all know, Alicia & Evan's beautiful second son was born on 3/17; very happy for them. As you also know, they have Marshall & their 'foster' daughter Juliana who is 7 weeks old. Much like my great-niece, Molly, Juliana is not interested in a car ride. Put her in the car seat & she's fine; put her in the car in the aforementioned car seat & holy moley - it's not pretty. According to my niece, she'll grow out of this; WHENNNNN????

I picked up Marshall & Juliana from Evan's parents today to drive the two kids to Howell to their Great-Aunt-Becca's. I kid you not, Juliana cried from about 2 miles north of Westphalia all the way to Howell. More than sixty minutes listening to a baby cry. Yes, I felt bad for her, yes, I wanted to pull over & snuggle with her, BUT I am also aware she cries in the car & ya just have to re-harden that already hardened heart & keep driving. Marshall - on the other hand - after about 15 minutes of singing in the backseat & ignoring the caterwauling, he proudly displayed his masculinity & went to sleep. He slept soundly for the next 45 minutes & would still be sleeping if I'd kept driving. Of course, Juliana would still be crying. Marshall woke up when I pulled into Rebecca & Barry's driveway & stopped the car, about the same time Juliana stopped crying. Do I see a life-long pattern here?

Blessed to have kids, grandkids, and great-grandkids and lucky to have so many people in their lives that love, and care, for them. But, I beg you - please no more driving a crying baby for an hour!!!! $20 says there's a crying kid in the plane sitting right by me tomorrow - assuming the plane takes off......I'm going to be disappointed if I'm not sitting on a beach amongst palm trees with a glass - hell, make it a barrel - of wine tomorrow night.

Oh yea, and my neurosurgeon appears to be a dope. He asked this morning "What did your doctor tell you?". Me: "That there's nothing more he can do & I need to see a neurosurgeon". Him: "Not sure yet if you need surgery, but that is all I do; he does everything else. What did he tell you?". My faith in the medical community is faltering.

TODAY I AM FEELING...

Grateful. Grateful for my immediate family & the relationships we share. Grateful for Alicia & Evan who took in her 1/2 sister & care so well for her & their sons. Grateful for my extended family who are in our lives. Grateful for my Mom and how she shows us ways to handle adversity. Grateful for my friends whether I see you once a week, once a month, once a year, or once a decade. Grateful even for our stupid dog who teaches us patience. Grateful for our neighbors that are also our friends. Grateful, especially, for Pete and the blessed life we share.

Blessed?? You say? Has she lost her mind? Well, being off all hormones & taking non-hormone therapy pills every day, that question is actually a yes. But we are blessed - read the above paragraph. Yes this has been a challenging few months but Becky no longer has melanoma, Jordan is getting through her treatments, my surgery was a success. While this all was indeed a challenge, it could be worse.

I am also grateful to finally be in Florida even though Madeira Beach sucks (more on that later). It is great to walk along the beach & watch the penguins - hell, told you I'd lost my mind - pelicans dive. Anyway, that's where I am today; love to all.

FL 2019 DAY 1 AND 2

The flight to Tampa was thankfully good. We had shipped fishing poles & some other crap to the UPS in St. Pete's so needed to be sure our rental car had the 'pull down' thing in the back seat so a long box could go into the trunk and go forward into the back seat. The guy at the car rental garage, said 'take any of the cars in that area' so we are looking for a car specifically with the aforementioned functionality. More than once, we thought we found one & it was just pull-down cup holders. I appreciate cup-holders but that was not what we needed. About the time the guy starts to approach us to see what was our problem, we found a vehicle that would work & were on our way.

Sorry to the Floridians & others that like this area but Treasure Island through Madeira Beach sucks. Condos, condo/motels, apartments, kitschy tourist shops, every chain restaurant known to mankind line both sides of the streets. Then you get to Remington Beach (we are right on the edge) & that's where the mansions line the ocean side of the street. Cute houses line the other side. Many of the cute house owners at some time added a second or third story porch to see the ocean over the original cute houses that lined the Oceanside. Now all they see are the mansions. This morning, I went for a walk going down the street side for a bit then walked along the ocean on my way back. I could see lights on in the mammoth homes but not one person was outside. I'm like - what in the dickens; I'd be enjoying my morning beverage on one of the many balconies on these places. Speaking of beverages, it is recycling day here & a lot of these wealthy people enjoy Stoli vodka & Captain Morgan's rum. Vodka & rum would be handy for where we are residing the next few days. As you all know, we cancelled our original trip except for Destin with our family next week. By the time, we decided to fly down, rental pickings were pretty slim. I reserved a room at this place & the owner called & asked if we'd take a smaller room as we were not reserving the entire week. Being affable, I said sure. Holy moley - this IS small. Really, really small. You enter the door & basically walk into a wall, trip over the enormous recliner, stub your toe on the dresser then see the bed is pushed up against the wall on one side. There is a teeny kitchen area & a teenier bathroom. The bathroom sink is in an alcove 20" wide (yes I measured it); people that are somewhat larger than Pete & I would not be able to access the bathroom sink. The side of the bed against the wall was, of course, 'my side', so I turned the nightstand on Pete's side of the bed, sideways (that's a lot of sides) then pushed the bed over which allows me about 10" to sidle along the wall to get into and out of bed. I also took the kitchen wastebasket, turned it upside down, placed it - of course sideways, covered it with a pillowcase & use it as a nightstand. I also put a towel on the floor by that side of the bed to wipe the sand off my feet before getting into bed. Our unit is the one closest to the road - the busy, busy, busy road. I was going to turn on the bathroom fan to cover that noise but alas, there is no bathroom fan (probably no room for it). Think I'm going to have to find a 'white noise' app. Also, there are lots of lights which shine in the window that doesn't open. Last night, I threw towels over the windows which helped a little. The room is small, but there are a lot of towels.

Including the overabundance of towels, there are some positives to this place. There is direct access to a nice beach. This is a 2 story condo-motel (whatever that is) and is right behind the last high-rise condo prior to Redington Beach. Walking back this morning along the beach, the high-rise condo easily marks where I leave the beach to return to our mini-me-room. We met 3 great couples last night that are staying here in much larger rooms. We talked with them quite a bit; they are from Wisconsin, Illinois, and Greenville, MI. Seems like a fun group; I'm sure we will be spending more time with them the next couple of days.

It's supposed to be cloudy & about 70 degrees today so this will be our exploring day. We were supposed to have spent 2 weeks down the road at Indian Rocks Beach so we will definitely check that out. Pete needs to get a fishing license as he is convinced there are hordes of fish to be caught in Destin. We will likely be looking for a mom & pop type bar/restaurant for supper rather than Sloppy Jo's, Joe's Crab Shack, Daiquiri Shak (spelled correctly) Starbucks, Hooters. Yea, Hooters is where I want to go: "I'd like to buy a pair of Hooters please".....

CAN'T MAKE THIS STUFF UP

Our time in our very cramped quarters was up yesterday, we were relieved to be moving out of there but will miss the great people we spent time with while there. A very nice, fun group of people; we have many great memories of being with them.

So...what can't be made up? One story we were told during happy hour was the couple who got married by a judge. This was during the time of the Star Wars popularity; the groom's son was 5. When they arrived in the court room, the son asked "Is Darth Vader going to marry you?".

In the room down from us, there was a couple who were here for a wedding; I don't remember their names, call them Julio and Tom. Tom joined our group for drinks and said the wedding guests were all attending a pre-wedding day sail on a yacht that evening. The wedding was on the beach the next day at 6:00 in the evening. Since I couldn't persuade him to bring me along on the yacht, I told Tom if he or Julio fell off the yacht, I'd be willing to go to the wedding with the survivor. This plays in later. We asked about Julio & Tom finally persuaded him to come out & say hi; Julio is a tad shy. We didn't see Julio or Tom at all the next day (no, they didn't fall off the boat). About 6:45, I'm walking by their door as Tom is approaching their room. I said "Aren't you supposed to be at a wedding?". Seems Tom got a tad drunk the prior night & after returning to the motel, went for a walk on the beach, got wild, someone called the cops & he'd been in jail all day. He claims he doesn't remember any of this; no reason not to believe him. As we proceed to his door, Julio opens the door & is very relieved to see Tom. Ends up Julio just sat in the room all day waiting for Tom to re-appear. I asked why he hadn't called the police & Tom replies that Julio is from Brazil. I told Julio that unlike Brazil, if you call the cops for help here, you typically don't disappear. The guys missed the wedding ceremony, Tom wanted to go to the reception, Julio was not at all interested in even leaving the room. I told Tom I could change & be ready in 10 minutes; he deferred & as far as we know, spent the rest of the night in his room. Pete says there is a lot more to that story.

I talked with my sister last night & she shared a story about Mimi. That dang dog just won't go away. Well, she almost did. The ice maker in Mom's kitchen refrigerator/freezer went on the fritz & she had water all over the floor. My brother lives a couple blocks away so Mom called him for help. He moved out the refrigerator, turned off the freezer part, they carried all the food in the freezer from the house to the garage freezer, cleaned up the mess & slid the fridge back into place. During this time, the door from the kitchen to the garage was open as well as the garage doors to the outside. My brother goes home, Mom can't find Mimi (not even in a pillowcase). She looked through the house, looked outdoors then called my brother that the dog was missing. Mom, my brother, the neighbor kids looked everywhere for that dog. It was getting dark & the search was called off for the evening. Mom searched the house again then called my brother & asked if it's possible the dog is behind the refrigerator. Just to placate her, he came back over a 3rd time, moved out the refrigerator, and out comes Mimi. I absolutely cannot stop laughing. I will admit it would have been awful in a couple weeks when Mom noticed a stench and found the matted remains of Mimi. We are in a hotel & can hear this yippy dog barking, I told Pete "If that thing doesn't shut up, it's going behind the refrigerator.".

Speaking of dogs, I get a phone call on Wednesday from a Steve from Fowler asking if I have a dog named Marley. I had told

Alicia & Evan there was no need to tie up Marley; I'd walked through their yard with her & I didn't think she'd leave the yard. Wrong. She went to visit Steve. She will now either be in a pen or tied up while outside during her stay with them. She's too big to keep behind a refrigerator.

The kids & 5 of the grandkids arrive in Destin today; very excited to spend a week with them. Alicia's not here so I needn't worry about someone dropping a bottle of blue liquor in the kitchen and seeing it splashed all over the white cupboards & the floor. Ellen, Alicia, Evan, Marshall, Juliana, & Harrison, we will miss you; hopefully you can join us on a future adventure.

SWIMSUITS

Before leaving home, I paid $60 to have 'swimboob' pockets sewn into 2 of my favorite swimsuits. Well, that doesn't work.

Both swimsuits are of the strapless variety; they originally came with a removable strap that I just tossed out. Ends up with the lightweight swim boobs in the pockets, it pulls the top down. Ends up taking out the boobs doesn't help because it was apparently the original ones that helped keep the top up. Ends up I wasted $60.

After seeing a few posts on assorted 'flat' websites, I looked for, and found, a ruffly swimsuit top. This works relatively well as the ruffles hide the concave area that were once breasts.

Back to the strapless swimsuits. I decided to break out the swim prosthesis, put them into the swimsuit & went out to the pool. It seemed a little loose but doable; things really got loose when I got in the pool & those prosthesis got wet. I was on a floaty chair & couldn't really jump off while hanging onto the top of my swimsuit. I pulled out the prosthesis & asked Ava (12) if she'd put them in the house. She took a teeny bit of each between her thumb & index finger & tossed them into the house. She later asked me if I could move her hat; I told her it was the least I could do. Ava is also the one who saw the scar under my arm & stated "Ewww, what is that??". I told her that was nothing, she should see the ones on my chest; she wasn't interested.

We are enjoying the weather; high 60's, low 70's & sunny. Pool is heated & a perfect temperature for the weather.

FL DAY WHATEVER IT IS

There are worse places to enter a new update than being in Destin, FL watching some of the grandkids swim in the pool. The grandkids have been somewhat hesitant about this mastectomy. As always, I am open and honest with them but they had not been ready to acknowledge it.

As of Tuesday after spending 3.5 days consecutive days with me, that all changed. I went to shoot baskets with Noah & Gavin. Gavin says "Don't knock your boobs off....oh, too late.". After I missed several baskets, Noah commented that I shot better when I had boobs. I told them I'd go put them on & see if it helps & they thought that would be a good idea. No, I am not offended by their jokes; I am encouraged by them. I've handled this with serious explanations as well as jokes; to me, joking has always helped with a bad situation & this is not an exception. I am pleased they can now feel free to kid with me about this.

Yesterday (on Wednesday), I thought about putting in the regular prosthesis but I was going to have to take them out of a bra & put them into a camisole. Let me tell you, this bra thing was a lot easier when the breasts were firmly affixed to my body. Anyway, I just couldn't be bothered so put the swim prosthesis into the camisole. Most of the time I don't bother with either but some shirts have those pesky darts & so, the prosthesis are pretty much required or I end up with pointy fabric sticking up; simply looks ridiculous. Later in the day, Ella & Ava were in my bedroom with me; I gave Ella a hug & she said "Gosh, those fake boobs are hard.". I explained they are the swim ones & the others were better & they were welcome to hold them. Surprisingly, both said yes so I pulled them out of the bra in the dresser & gave them to the girls. Some may think "WTH"; my thoughts are if I can make them more comfortable with this & for anyone else in the future who may have breast cancer, it is positive progress.

Not positive is Marley dog who is struggling with getting up the 3 steps at Alicia & Evan's. Alicia sent a message asking for donations for a wheelchair & a ramp for the dog. I think just a ramp would suffice.

What isn't sufficient is the electric golf cart that comes with this house rental. It tends to run out of 'juice'. Yesterday, us 6 adults were on it & literally had to push it back. Pete & Barry are in the back pushing, Brad is using his left foot to push (sort of Fred Flintstone style), Tricia decides to jump off to take a picture of them, trips & lands in the grass cutting her ankle (no stitches needed, thx for asking). Rebecca & I decided to just sit there & let others handle it. Yes, alcohol was involved (except Rebecca).

Hey - have a good day; gotta go swim - sans boobs.

STILL IN FLORIDA

The kids & grandkids headed home yesterday (Saturday, 3/30); Pete & I are in St. George Island, FL last night & tonight then head to Tampa to fly home Tuesday. Thanks to our family for a great week in Destin; it was a fun 7 days with only 3, well maybe 5 injuries. Noah cut the top of his big toe on the roughest parking lot ever, Gavin had Xrays to be sure he had not re-broken his toes, Tricia's previously mentioned ankle & Brad and Barry coming in at #4 & 5 as each had sore ankles after playing basketball. Brad probably hurt his ankle when he was carrying Noah out from under the basket; I can't say for certain that is an unsportsmanlike activity but I've never seen it done in any other basketball game.

St. George Island....I'm grateful our winter vacation plans had to be changed or we would have been here for a week. A lll-loooonnnngggg week. The upside of this Island is there are no go-cart tracks, no miniature golf, no arcades, very few souvenir stores. The downsides include only 4 bars & not a lot to do. Both Madeira Beach & Destin have beautiful turquoise water & wonderful soft sandy beaches; I'm happy to sit at the beach & look at the water. St. George Island is pebbly tan sand & grayish water. Madeira Beach & Destin have sidewalks and many pedestrian crosswalks. St. George Island - you pretty much take your life in your own hands to walk anywhere. There is a bike/walking trail from one end of the island to the other but other than that sidewalks are few & far between & crosswalks are virtually non-existent. We can cross off our list a return trip here. By the way, the island is very dog-friendly; accommodations, restaurants, beaches all welcome them. Good place if you want to spend time bonding with your dog.

I texted Alicia & Evan to see how their family & our dog are doing. She replied that Marshall had fed Marley some cheese puffs (a big no-no) and shortly thereafter Marley regurgitated the cheese puffs over Marshall's hot wheel cars. I asked her how many cars she threw away.

Remember Monday is April Fool's Day so don't believe everything you are told tomorrow.

FLIGHT HOME AND ARRIVING HOME

To quote the flight attendant "This is the weirdest flight ever.". Cats, dogs, birds, you name it, it was probably on that flight.

Bless their hearts, there were 12-15 non-mobile senior citizens flying from Tampa to Grand Rapids. May we all be lucky enough to do this in our futures. And absolutely bless the Frontier staff that had to transport all of them through the huge Tampa airport to their seats in the airplane. Needless to say, this was very time-consuming.

It was also time-consuming for one hapless employee who had to round up the buggy-eyed chihuahua in a pink dress when its' owner for some reason let it out of its' zippered case. That thing sped out of the cage like a horse starting the KY Derby & had no intention of being returned to its' crate. This is the same woman who thought a little boy was her grandson; she kept trying to get the kid to come to her & he simply clung to his Dad. Again, bless her. I completely sympathize with those with Alzheimers or Dementia; we have family members with both but all the same sometimes you think "Holy Cow!".

So, it takes some time to get all those with physical or mental issues on the plane; then one of the ladies had to use the bathroom so they had to hold up the line while they transported her to & from the restroom. As we walked into the plane, I told one of the transporters "Thank you for your help & patience". We finally board & someone was in our seats; the stewardess told us they "couldn't sit in the front row" so they had to move them, just take the seats across the aisle. OK fine but this did cause further confusion for the people whose seats into which we were placed. Pete & I were towards the front of the plane and watched as a couple more crated dogs were brought in as well as one on a leash that simply wanted to get under everyone's seat (service dog my butt). Then the lady who had the seat across the aisle from us arrived with the biggest cat you've ever seen! The kid sitting next to me asked "Do you see the size of that thing?". I told him I wished I had a mouse. Just an aside here: Lots of people are allergic to peanuts, lots of people are allergic to cats. We were on a flight once when we were told someone had a peanut allergy so no peanut products would be served; how about all the people on the plane allergic to cats??? Or dogs, or birds.... Back to the story at hand. One of the flight attendants walks up front & asks the other "Dogs, a cat & birds in a box. Where do we put the birds?". I'm thinking "Next to the cat".

An interesting note for those of you that may fly Frontier in the future. Sit in at least row 5 if you have items to be stowed in the overhead bins. The bins over row 1 are reserved for the safety crap so those in row 1 must store their stuff over row 2, row 2 goes over row 3 or further & so on. So those of us in rows 1 through at least 3 (9 people) must have those in the further rows take down our items and hand them from one person to another until they reach us. Fortunately those on the return flight were the type to laugh with us about it & gladly help. On our flight down the crabby guy wasn't so pleasant.

We arrive home, turn the water back on, Pete flushes the toilet in the 1/4 bathroom & water flies out everywhere. Welcome home. Busy week with the assorted physicians; today I have an appointment with my family doctor as the U of M turned down her referral for my back as I had not seen her specifically for my back for a couple months. I then have my monthly blood draw for liver enzymes. Tomorrow we go to the U of M to meet my new oncologist. Friday I have OMM on my back followed by the 2 phase bone scan insurance insisted on before they authorize the additional blood test to try to find out why the bone marrow in my lower back has edema. Next week, I have genetic testing for breast cancer because with the testing done with Rebecca, they only tested her for cancer, not me. No idea why. Saturday, we will be going to Flushing to celebrate Pete's brothers 76th birthday; Pete's 71st is Monday. No idea what we are doing for his birthday, probably hiding.

WHERE HAVE I BEEN?

It has been a whirlwind since we got home Tuesday. Between the doctor appointments, medical tests, and birthday party, I'm still not done completely unpacking. With one trip over, I am planning our late September trip to Ireland, Scotland, and Amsterdam. More on that in a bit.

My appointment with the U of M oncologist was great - a weird term when discussing cancer but nonetheless Pete & I were both very pleased with Dr. Cobain (the oncologist), Dr. Schwartz (the resident) and Andrea (the PA). You may recall I had been told it was impossible to tell if the cancer in the right breast was a separate cancer or if it had metastasized from the right side. Dr. Cobain said it was separate because while both of them were 100% estrogen, the progesterone percentages were different. This, actually, is good news. She is fine with the Letrozole for non-HRT but said monthly liver enzyme tests are not needed & suggests I start taking Zometa for the Osteopenia. I see her again in 3 months which is when I'll start taking the Zometa. Moving forward from that, I will see her every six months. One thing we didn't expect is to hear is that the non-HRT treatment is only 50% effective in stopping a recurrence. WTH??? She said adding Zometa adds another 2%. Guess I'll take all the increased percentages I can get.

The bone scan I had on Friday was to be only for my back but the radiologist - bless her - suggested that since I was recently diagnosed with breast cancer that they do the entire body. She obtained permission from the doctor & we proceeded with the full body bone scan. Nothing to do on my part but lay there longer. Kind of weird that they put a band around your feet;

it's supposed to help you hold still. I couldn't help but think if there's a fire alarm, I'll be hopping out of there like Harvey the Rabbit. When I think about it though, I don't think Harvey hopped.

Let's hop back (eye roll here) to our September-October trip. I started making reservations this morning & did 3 out of the 4 wrong including having booked us on the wrong island. Causing part of my confusion is that the European calendar is Monday-Sunday not Sunday-Saturday so the days of the week are in the "wrong" square. The other part of the confusion is simply me being me.

Hope y'all have a good week.

CLOTHING

I think it may be easier to become a nudist. This morning, I went through my closet, tried everything on & sorted it into 3 categories: "No Boobs OK", "Needs Boobs", and "Good God, give it away!".

Fortunately the "No Boobs OK" category has the most items. Tops with a draped neckline definitely need a camisole to be worn under them. The things people don't tell you; I am adding my clothing comments to my list "Simple Things You Should Know about a Mastectomy".

Today is Pete's birthday, later today we are going to Top Golf in Auburn Hills. I will soon let you know if I golf better without breasts. I might make it on the LPGA yet.

GETTING OLD

Just so you know, I am referencing myself and my dog.

Marley used to be on a very expensive dog food due to her rather sensitive stomach. When Marley spent time with my son's family in the Spring of 2018, she wolfed down their dogs' (plural, pretty sure it isn't dogs's') food with no side effects so we switched her to Purina Senior Dog Food. Today I searched 2 different stores for this Senior Dog Food and could not find it. I finally see a revised bag stating Adult 7+. For heaven's sakes, now we have to be politically correct about a DOG's age???? It's no longer acceptable for a bag to say "Senior" Dog Food. Maybe everyone else's dog is way smarter than ours but to-date, our dog has not yet learned to read. Per those that study these things, she sees in black & white and doesn't even know the color of the bag has changed; she'll eat whatever slop is in her bowl. Give me a break "Adult 7+"......

Holy crap, it is windy! Our Christmas tree has been awaiting its' demise in a 'burn' pile since around December 29th; it's blown half way to the river! You are thinking "What's that got to do with getting old?". Not a dang thing, I just happened to look out the window. Squirrel!!!

Now, Down South, it is a sign of respect to call a woman "Ma'am". In the Northern regions, it is reserved for those of us no longer as fresh as we once were. The first time I was called Ma'am was in a grocery store & I was appalled; the second time was in a bar & I told the bartender it would be less offensive to be called bitch. Yes, I know that is a female dog but nonetheless. If I'd been a dog I would have been given a drink for those age 49+.

Like my dog, I am - well, have - turned grey. I used to color my hair or have it professionally highlighted & when I had to start carrying a color stick with me on vacations, I decided enough was enough. My hairdresser told me I would not be pleased with the color. Horse hockey, she wanted the money. I switched to someone else who patiently took a year to get my tresses to their natural grey. During that timeframe, our eldest grand-daughter, who was 17 at the time, colored her hair "platinum". We had the exact same hair color. I am SO trendy (roll of the eyes). OK - just be patient. When we were in Florida, my 'beach sandal's broke so I went into a store to buy a new pair. I'm walking around with the box (and the shoes in the box) & ended up chatting with one of the sales people. She said "Everyone is coming in asking for BrandName shoes". I told her I had no idea what those are; she replied "You are holding them". Yup, I'm a real trendsetter. Squirrel!!

Another wonderful side of aging is back issues have become more prevalent; when we were in Florida in 2018, my back went out. Spasming like crazy. When you see someone walking slowly because their back hurts & you think "It can't be that bad", you just wait. It is worse than labor. For you men out there, it is worse than a paper cut. We were staying in a second floor unit. Marley & I were like two 150-year olds trying to get up those steps. Her hips aren't great & my back was worthless. My husband finally said, that's it, we are going home early. Nothing like a 1200 mile car ride with one's back in spasms.

Marley's knees are still looking pretty good - I just had to look at her to be sure dogs have knees; they do, but they are backwards. Mine are getting old & wrinkly. They look like freakin' huge prunes. WTH. On the bright side, I'll never have breasts that look like prunes....the benefits of a double mastectomy. BTW, for you with still attractive knees - put your knees together real tight & take a picture - looks like a butt. Really.

Well, I could go on & I will in another chapter. Right now it is 5:55 pm or if you prefer military time, it is 1755 & it is way past Happy Hour.

GRASS NOT GROWING UNDER OUR FEET!

This week I finalized our trip to Ireland, Scotland & Amsterdam. You may recall we were supposed to go to Scotland last year for Pete's birthday but it was cancelled because he had bowel resection surgery. We (well, I) decided to add 2 more countries this time. Everything, except a plan for the dog, is ready for that trip this Fall.

I then booked Florida & Spring Break for 2020. Brad, Tricia & 3 of their daughters will be joining Tricia's parents in Clearwater Beach next year so the rest of us (except Ellen due to school) will be going to Hilton Head. Pete & I will spend part of February & the last full week of March in Florida. Marley will be with Pete & I in Florida and I've found an in-home doggy day care for her in Hilton Head. That dog should be grateful, I had to pass on some lodging because there was more than 1 step or several steps & no elevator. I cannot believe I am selecting accommodations based on the dog's needs. She'd best still be alive next February. (In case you are wondering Brad & Tricia's family will be back with us in 2021.)

I just booked a trip to Turks & Caicos for January 2020!! I looked at various islands yesterday & believe it or not, this is late to make a January reservation so partly due to availability, I chose Turks & Caicos. Pete gets up this morning & I tell him I believe we will be going to Turks & Caicos; first he'd heard of this plan.

Bless his heart, 6 hours later, I had us fully booked. For whatever reason, we got away from major traveling & after this slightly bothersome cancer, I'm back all over that. We are very excited to be visiting a new location. Marley will be staying in Michigan for this trip. Hurry & get in line for requesting to keep the dog in late September/early October or/and in January as I'm sure people will be clamoring to watch her. Since being on Synthroid, her shedding is much less, she doesn't drool much, and she is housebroken. (Same could be said of me.)

For all of these adventures, I plan to leave my prosthesis at home. I have to thank my niece Beth for sending me the cartoon with the woman taking off her bra & her prosthesis falling on the floor. In this age of overdone political correctness, I am happy there are those that know me & know they can feel comfortable sending me something like that. I am pleased to know it is realized I will not be offended & will find it funny. Keep a sense of humor, people!

WELL!

We are going out tonight & I have on a shirt I thought was suitable with a camisole under it. Pete just said "Wearing a low-rider???". Guess I'll go change my clothes and hang this one with the "Boobs Required" garments.

SHOPPING

After my beloved husband commented on my shirt yesterday, I decided to shop for some new ones. I will admit shopping is one of the things that kind of takes my breath away. Not because I am not an avid shopper, I'm not, but it's quite a change to have to look for shirts with 'gathers' and multi-patterns. I'll see a shirt & think "Oh, that's cute" then realize the fabric will cling to my concave areas; figures that wouldn't be my stomach. The Fates can be cruel.

As you know, I had to shop for a different swimsuit in Florida & during that expedition, I also looked at dresses and shirts. It's just a different experience; imagine shopping for a hat without a head. Well, without a head, you'd have a whole host of other issues: couldn't see to drive, can't order fast food through the speaker, no where to put your sunglasses.....wouldn't really need that hat. Without breasts, oddly enough, one typically still needs clothes. I had told a friend that the prosthesis weren't working so great & she suggested buying a thickly padded bra. I'm strolling through a store today poking at the bras to see which ones wouldn't collapse on contact. I left before Security kicked me out.

On a very bright note, my new license plate came in today. It is a breast cancer license plate with the letters BAOR (Boobs are OverRated). It's simply dashing on the back of the car with the palm tree license plate holder I ordered the other day. Clothes be damned; I have an awesome license plate.

MASTECTOMY TIPS AND TECHNIQUES

Some of these are from U of M's website, some are from a friend that had a mastectomy a few years back, most are just unfortunate personal experience.

Pre-mastectomy

- If at all possible, choose a surgeon that specializes in breast cancer vs a general cancer surgeon. Ditto for the oncologist.

- If mammogram was clear & cancer was later found in one breast via an ultrasound or MRI, insist on having an ultrasound or MRI on the other side before surgery.

- Start the exercises they give you for post-surgery so you know how to do them and how they feel.

- If you don't have one, get an oral thermometer.

- Unless you have someone at home to clean your house while you recuperate, hire a house cleaner.

- Freeze some meals.

- Have ice packs ready; you will need at least two.

- You will not be able to reach up high for at least a week, if you have anything in your cupboards above chest level that you will need, move them now.

- If you attended a breast clinic, you may have been given a small pillow – bring that to the hospital with you as you will need it under the seatbelt strap on the way home. Otherwise, buy a soft, pliable one.

- Order a wedge pillow for your bed as it is uncomfortable to lay flat. You will also need your regular head pillow & 2 small ones to place on either side of you to rest your arms. Some people opt to sleep in a recliner, I preferred my own bed & the wedge pillow was perfect (can purchase on Amazon).

- I was told to buy a post-mastectomy camisole; these have pockets to hold the drains. I found the camisole to be horribly uncomfortable and used it only to hold the drains while I showered. After the surgery, I discovered there are lightweight shirts that you can buy that have 'drain bulb' pockets in them. I ended up just pinning the drains into my shirts. If you plan to do this, or think you may, be sure you have safety pins.

- Speak of showers, get a shower chair, you are going to want it.

- Buy some very lightweight, very soft button down shirts. Be sure the buttons are small & light. I first bought some cotton button down shirts at Goodwill that felt soft enough at the time but against post-surgery skin, you're going to want something lighter than cotton.

- The shirts can also be used for pj's; if you'd rather have pajama's – the same as the shirts – lightweight, soft and button-down.

- Buy "yoga type" pants

- Fuzzy socks are nice – be sure they have the little rubber grippy things so you don't slip.

- Move a table/nightstand next to the side of your bed with anything on it you may want or need: water, lip balm, book, tissues, lamp, etc

- Make a list of people to contact with the results of your surgery (friends/family/co-workers/neighbors/whomever)

- 4x4 gauze pads & tape to cover the incisions for your drain tubes.
- A method of exercising at home, ie a step to go up & down, a treadmill, a gazelle (the exercise thing, not the animal), something to keep you moving post-surgery.
- Very soft lightweight camisoles without a 'bra tray'. At the time I had my surgery, Jockey Enhance Supersoft were wonderful; these can be ordered in a multitude of colors on-line.

Take to the Hospital
- Phone/ipad/charger
- Tissues
- Chapstick
- Lipstick
- Face/Body Creams
- Book or electronic reader i.e. Nook
- Clothes to wear home – be sure to have a button down shirt
- The little pillow referenced earlier

Post-mastectomy
- When the hospital offers you a stool-softener, take it or you will be very sad that you did not. Apparently the pain killers cause constipation.
- Your incision will be far longer than you thought. I did a double mastectomy and the incisions extend from the middle of my chest to just under my arm. There's about ¾" between the middle incisions. You will be swollen and black & blue.
- If you have a sentinel node biopsy, this is the sorest incision. Weird because your breasts have just been removed but the area of the biopsy is much more tender.

- Watch your posture. For whatever reason, after this surgery, one tends to list forward.

- About the time your incisions start to feel better, your chest may feel like it is on freakin' fire. Apparently this is from the nerves healing; nobody told me about this. It doesn't happen to everyone but it is pretty awful when it occurs. I tried ice packs, Benadryl Cooling Spray, and Aloe. I also tried BioFreeze but that stung; it may work for you, just try on a small area first or you may be galloping to the shower.

- You will need a garment to wear in the shower to hold your drains; I used the unzipped camisoles mentioned above. Some people use a lanyard.

- Prior to taking a shower, be sure your shampoo/conditioner, soap, razors, shaving cream are within reach while sitting on the shower chair.

- Be aware that by the time you empty the drains, get undressed & are ready to shower, you may need a short break before actually showering.

- If you rest your drain bulbs on the counter after emptying them, do not move until you re-attach them to your garment.

- Be mindful of your drain tubes when pulling up your pants; they tend to want to get caught inside.

- Do your arm exercises twice a day.

- Some days you will feel good, others you will feel worn out. Don't fret, listen to your body.

- It is recommended to walk for exercise; the people recommending this obviously do not understand minus10 windchills in the winter. As already mentioned, have some sort of exercise equipment available.

- As you heal, the shirts that previously felt good may

be bothersome as they move against your body – this is why you bought the lightweight camisoles. Now is the time to put them under your shirt.

- Sheets & blankets can be slightly painful against your skin. After about 2 weeks, my skin was very sensitive to touch so I'd unbutton the pajama shirt at night, open it up & had the bed coverings at my waist. Would've scared the bejeesus out of any burglar that would have wandered into the house. I had this surgery in the winter, in Michigan so it was cold. One night I have the top unbuttoned & it's getting caught under me so I figured I'd just take it off (drains were out at this point). Then my arms got cold & I had to put the shirt back on.

- Tell people 'no hugs'; you will not want any for a while.

- If you are not doing reconstruction (or I guess if you are & are a different size), sort through your clothes: 1) Flat 2) Needs Prosthesis 3) Give Away

- When buying new tops or dresses & you are wearing them 'flat', don't buy anything with darts; it just looks funky.

- I don't know if it is really doing anything, but I started putting Vitamin E oil on my incisions about 4 weeks after surgery.

- Be kind to yourself & keep a sense of humor.

- Let's talk about prosthesis. I, well my insurance, purchased a pair of Amoena Essential Light which I obtained at a great mastectomy store near my home. If you had a single breast removed, this is definitely the way to go. If you had a double mastectomy, allow me to recommend Athleta Empower Pads. The Amoena set feels much like a normal breast, the thing I didn't like is the weight of them. A very structured bra is needed to keep these in place & I found the bras un-comfortable. I tried sports-type bras but within a few hours, they had stretched out so the prosthesis were much lower than where one's 'real' breasts had resided. The beauty of the Athleta Empower Pads is they are lightweight & easily fit into any sports bra with a pocket, Jockey & an online company called 'handful' both carry sports bras with pockets. The Empower Pads can be ordered online for $20.00 for 2 sets; the Amoena prosthesis were > $800.00 for a pair. While purchasing the Amoena ones, I also got a pair for swimming. These didn't work so good as they tend to pull down the swimsuit. Instead of using those, I bought a swimsuit top with tiered ruffles. Dang swim-suit tops cost almost as much as the swim prosthesis :)

FRONT OF BODY GOOD, BACK OF IT NOT SO MUCH

For you rude ones out there, I'm referring to my actual back not my bootie. Although at 63, my bootie is decidedly not as pretty as it was maybe a decade or so ago :) You may recall I had a 3-Phase Bone Scan the other week. Saw our friendly neurologist Thursday afternoon. We already had the report which does not use little words. I tried looking stuff up on the internet but whenever I referenced "Moderately intense uptake...", the internet kept taking me to sites for PET scans. For PET scans, those 3 words in quotes can mean cancer. Not so in a 3-Phase Bone Scan.

Since I can still read, I was able to peruse my report prior to the appointment but as referenced above, I certainly did not understand it. Eighty minutes or so past our appointment time, the doctor came in, I asked him what the report means. To quote him: "Delayed static images demonstrate moderately focal uptake....may be related to treated discitis/osteomyletis and/or discogenic subcholdral osseous reactive changes". Well no shit, dickweed, I was able to read that by myself. "See Jane Run, See Dick Run, See Spot Run, See Jane Smack Doctor....." (You youngsters won't understand that sentence.) I then asked if he could please explain what the report means. He said well, for this test, the radioactive material is not supposed to go into the bone but it did on a portion of my back. He said it is not metastatic (i.e. cancer - good thing), the bone marrow edema found on the

MRI with contrast could be caused by an infection or arthritis. Basically, they don't have a clue what is causing the back pain & I have another MRI in June. Based on that, they may do a biopsy or a culture. Apparently this doctor does not feel the patient should be informed as to which type of biopsy or culture; if it is needed, I'll find out specifics & make a decision then. My appointment with U of M for my back isn't until August 1st so I'll continue with the current neurologist till then; figure the more testing done before I get to the U of M, the more information they'll have before my appointment.

Let's see - anything else new? Jordan had the last scheduled Chemo treatment this past Wednesday; hopefully it is all uphill for Jordan from here. Rebecca continues to have unmelted stitches pop through her what-we-thought-was healed incision. I finally trapped that darned red squirrel that's been eating my Mother Hen & Chicks plants for the last 2 summers. Took that little fella on a big ride.

APOLOGIES IF NEEDED

I have stated that my mastectomy and cancer were no big deal. I do not mean in any way to infer that breast cancer is no big deal as it is very traumatic. My statement of 'no big deal' is that in comparison to Jordan's ordeal and a classmate's continuing breast cancer treatment, a mastectomy was easy. No hair loss, no being sick for days every few weeks, no side effects (known and unknown), I cannot complain.

As I've stated before, I honestly do not feel as if I've had cancer. I was stunned by Jordan's and Rebecca's cancers so I was already on overload when I heard of mine. Then the surgery was within two weeks so I really had no time to ponder the cancer before the surgery was already completed. Poof, done. Poof, because of a shoe, Cinderella is a princess. Poof, because of cancer, I am without breasts. Big difference is for me, nothing changes at midnight. That's a good thing as I don't need mice running through my bed. (Sorry, can't help myself.)

I offer sincerest apologies to anyone I may have offended by making light of **my** cancer. I am not in any way indicating that breast cancer is anything other than very serious & life-changing. I am blessed that I got out of it so easily in comparison to thousands of others. If I act as if my experience was rough, I will feel that I would be discounting those that are going through the difficulties of chemo, radiation, and the side effects. I simply cannot do that; I pray every day that God helps them & their families through their trials.

WHERE HAVE I BEEN?

Excellent question. Been busy.

Took Mom's dog to the groomer & took Mom to the Secretary of State to renew her driver's license. She passed her eye exam with flying colors – referencing Mom here. Lots of people complain about the Secretary of State branch offices (in Michigan, that's where you go to get driver's licenses, license plates, etc); yes, it can be excruciatingly slow but it is not necessarily the employees who are to be blamed. The people who show up with incorrect papers or they left their papers in the car or they can't answer the easy questions such as "Who is your doctor?". No, I do not know why that question was asked of this particular customer but it was overheard. In any event, Mimi is groomed, Mom is licensed to drive & her vehicle has the 2019-2020 tabs on it.

Another item we had to address this week and she keeps turning up like a bad penny, is Alicia & Ella's horrid mother. As you know, she had another baby born on drugs (3 known of 6) & Juliana is thriving with Alicia & Evan. Court was on Friday; that damned Angie is the biggest freaking liar in the world. Anyway, her counselor of 2 months at the methadone clinic testified how Angie is trying so hard blah blah blah. Never mind she's been going there for two years without moving forward; all of a sudden she is wonder woman. Angie gets up to testify and now claims that when Caroline (now around 8) was born with drugs in her system, it's because Angie was in a vehicle with Sam (the Dad of Caroline) who was smoking marijuana. WTF!!!! This is news, after all the other court dates this excuse is now coming up – pleeeeease. I looked this up & one needs to be in an enclosed, unventilated space for an hour with the marijuana having a percentage > 13.5% or something close to that. Mya, who had heroin in her system, was delivered in an ambulance. Must be the paramedics were shooting up & accidentally injected Mya. Angie also claims she is living in Lansing although it is really Muir; she couldn't provide the correct zip code for the Lansing address but hey – let's all believe the lying, toothless blob. If she were to give her correct address, she would be in Ionia County CPS which are the ones that took away the other six kids. She wants to stay in Ingham County as for whatever reason Ionia County can't share their info with Ingham County. If this case was in Ionia County, her parental rights would have already been terminated. They said she seems to be bonding with Juliana in her twice weekly 2 hour visits & was seen rubbing the baby's back & singing to her. Big f'n deal; I could rub an orangatan's back & sing to it for 4 measly hours a week. So, Angie gets another 90 days to try to stay off drugs and if she does, she gets Juliana in late July. She's stayed off drugs a couple other times for 6 months but always goes back to them. This will be no different. We are all horribly upset, especially Alicia & Ella who had to be with their mother as younger children. We are all sending documentation to the Judge, the Prosecutor, and CPS. I also think I am sending it to the counselor at Victory Services – oh, she has a certificate to do counseling. I'm sure she is great. If there's an attorney out there that wants to do some pro-bono work, Alicia & Evan could certainly use your help. Angie sits up there & lies, her counselor is bizarre in her testimony & nobody questions it. Trust me, I have a very hard time sitting there & not standing up yelling "Bullcrap, let me tell you the truth". Here's another good one; Angie was booted out of Sparrow hospital because Juliana's drug level went up & it is suspected Angie snuck in breast milk. Ya see, the longer the baby is in the hospital with drugs, the longer the mother has to get off them. What a wonderful mom to share her drugs with a newborn, we should all be so lucky. Angie's brilliant attorney said kicking

Angie out of the hospital was revenge. Revenge? Sparrow Hospital kicked her out for revenge, not for sneaking drugs to an infant??? Gosh, we all are so stupid. And, Alicia is keeping the baby for revenge on how her mother treated Alicia. Alicia is fostering that baby in the hopes of saving her from the life she & the other five kids had with Angie. Nope, revenge. Heavens forbid Angie would take any responsibility. Breaks my heart. Anyway, again if there is an attorney that can do some pro-bono work to save Juliana from going to her mother, it would be wonderful.

Also wonderful, possibly, is I am attending Bear - geesh BEER Yoga this afternoon. I can hardly wait :) Beer Yoga, I'm anticipating, will be fun. Bear Yoga - not so much. Let ya know how the Beer Yoga works out - sure hope I didn't misread that sign.

BEER YOGA

Ends up bear yoga may have been better for me. I cannot believe I am saying this but apparently - for me - alcohol, deep breathing & stretching simply do not go together. In full disclosure, I readily admit I wasn't ready for a beer at noon on Sunday so I ordered a Bloody Mary. That Bloody Mary & my stomach did not become friends. I drank less than 1/2 of it and left Beer Yoga with a belly ache.

Along with driving, operating a chainsaw, running heavy equipment, tying my shoes, climbing ladders, etc, I will add yoga to the list of things not to do while imbibing in adult beverages.

Enjoy your day.

INTIMACY

....or the lack thereof. Some of you may wish to skip this post as I'm sharing more than even I typically share but it may help someone somewhere avoid this. Not avoid intimacy, silly; read on if you dare.

I have mentioned that after my double mastectomy, I told people 'no hugs' for weeks. I could barely stand having fabric touch me much less another human. Or for that matter, a dog, a cat, a cow, a dinosaur, etc. I forget how many weeks it was before I didn't need to be enclosed in my pillow fortress at night. So, after several weeks, my spouse & I decide to get back into physical relations. Ow, ow, ow, WTF!!!!

Ends up women of a certain age experience 'vaginal shut down' if not taking any hormones. I'm no longer taking hormones and let me tell you, that thing was tighter than two fingers stuck together with Crazy Glue. I did my research and found it was recommended to try K-Y Gel. I warned you not to read this!!! Well, thank God for self-checkout lanes. There are a number of items I can purchase without embarrassment; not so K-Y. So that I wouldn't have to make this purchase again any time soon, I purchased two different types. In retrospect, I should have bought the entire shelf of it & stored it in the basement. Let's move on.

Try #1: About 45 seconds into it, I told Pete "You are not going to hear this often but wrap this up.".

Try #2: About 75 seconds.

Try #3: I got smart this time and applied the gel to Pete instead of me so the gel could be where it needed to be. Seems to work better but we are still in the experimentation stage.

Bottom line is I don't know what you can do to prevent this occurring while you heal; look it up & do your own damned research :) Do expect pain & bleeding but with you & your partner having a sense of humor, persistence & the correct gel, that will subside & you will get through this. Now the song "Feels Like the First Time" by Foreigner can zip through your head all day. When it does, you can say "Ewww".

NEVER THOUGHT I'D BE DOING THIS...

So far 2019 has proven to be a pain in the butt. Didn't think I'd ever be going to an oncologist with my daughter, never thought I'd be undergoing a double mastectomy, never thought 3 family members would have cancer at the same time, never thought I'd be dealing with completely worthless Angie again and I sure as hell never thought I'd get 'fitted' for golf clubs.

I know – right?!? Of the five items listed above, I am quite certain that those of you that know me well will be surprised the most at the golf club news. They aren't as pretty as I would have preferred but they have some nice scroll work on the 'stick' part. I had my choice of black & grey or black & blue; figured I'm usually bruised somewhere so went with the black & blue. They came with a bag but my old one is better (more pockets) so I am using that one. Pete commented the old bag is awful heavy. Re-reading that sentence, he dang well have been talking about the golf bag, not me.

While I can have weight issues, the golf bag was very heavy. I went through the pockets and found a blue ice pack thing, a full bottle of water, a 1/4 bottle of suntan lotion, and 1/2 of a fifth of Captain Morgan's Spiced Rum. Taking those out dropped the weight about ten pounds. (I figure taking off my shoes & earrings when I get weighed at the doctor has that same effect.) My golf shoes were also in the bag but they are very lightweight. My 'hitting' balls and the 'water' balls were in there. Missing in action are the little bag in which I kept my tees, ball markers, bandaids, chapstick, mini pads, tissues, corkscrew, matches, hand wipes, etc and my jacket. Wonder if I washed the jacket & hung it up somewhere......More likely, one of the grandkids wore it home. I have lost many pajama bottoms, sweatshirts, and zippered jackets to the 3 oldest granddaughters. They're like "I forgot a jacket, can I borrow one? Ooohh, that's soft.". And it's the last I see of that article of clothing.

Speak of clothing, – Oops, I'll have to get back to you. It's shuffleboard night & we need to leave. The shuffleboard in a bar on a long table, dummy, not the old person kind with the sticks. Good night.

BOY, I AM.....

...crabby! Even I can't stand being around me. The washer is dinging, I have to run downstairs; I cannot even get the washing machine to leave me the hell alone.

I'm back. Let's see, last week, I babysat Marshall, Juliana, and Harrison so Alicia could sell stuff in the annual town-wide garage sales. Nothing quite like changing 3 poopy diapers in 15 minutes. Angie's Mom, Chris, & Angie's Aunt Shelley & I tag-teamed the babysitting duties. Chris and I have always been polite with each other but with everything that has gone on over the years, we have found ourselves on opposite sides and sometimes struggle with that. I've never really sat down with Aunt Shelley. Last Friday afternoon, the 3 of us spent a few hours together watching the kids & checking on the sales and actually had a good time together. Ends up Aunt Shelley has a wicked sense of humor. Who would have thunk it??? I am proud of both Chris and I that throughout the struggles with Angie, we have never been outright rude to each other and are able to move beyond all of this when needed. It makes it easier for us & the entire extended family.

I took Marshall for a walk that Friday afternoon; had a bit of a struggle getting his shoes on. I noticed he was walking sort of weird during our outing but, what's a girl to do? We get back to their house and found the shoes that actually fit him. The ones he had on were probably an inch short. Sorry about that Mar-

shall

I sent a 6-page letter to the judge who is overseeing the case of Juliana's breeders (sure as heck am not calling them parents). I explained I've known Angie over 22 years, my knowledge of her lack of any maternal skills, and the fallacies she told during her testimony on April 24th, 2019. I don't know if it will make a difference but our hearts will break if Juliana goes to Angie or Andy. Ella wrote a great letter & that is being sent later today. Others are also sending letters to the judge; if anyone needs that address, let me know.

Went to the dermatologist today for the rash on my chest and left arm. It isn't shingles, it isn't caused by the Letrozole, trying a steroid cream for a couple of weeks to see what that does with it.

Got on the scales, gained back 4 of the 16 pounds I lost. Go off a diet for 2 days & boom; might be why I'm feeling cranky. Patty, Cyndy, & Joyce – I TOLD you I didn't want the potatoes!!!!!

In the bird department, yes apparently we have one, our male & female orioles are back, the rose-breasted grosbeak is back, the dang bluebirds have returned. Bluebird of happiness, my butt, those things are mean!!!

Over the years, I have watched 7 grandkids and now 3 great-grandkids go through various temper-tantrums. If we don't get a warm, sunny day soon, I may use their examples and throw a fit. It'll probably end up being a Rain Dance.

TAKE IT EASY?

Apparently there is a concept out there that while someone is getting over a cold/flu/sinus infection/whatever to take it easy a day or so when one starts feeling better. Huh?

Those of you on Facebook know I've had this cold thing since last week, soon my teeth started hurting. My teeth hurting always means a sinus infection so I got an antibiotic After 3 bouts of the antibiotic, I was starting to feel pretty good.

The neighbors were having a bonfire Saturday night so Pete, I and 2 of the grandkids went over & had a good time. Woke up Sunday, felt fine. Late Sunday afternoon I went out and transplanted a bunch of flowers, put out 5 bags of mulch & was thinking "Ha, I'm doing pretty good.". Slept 12 hours last night & feel like crap again today.

My sympathetic husband didn't mention that perhaps I did too much yesterday – Right! I've been reminded at least 3 times this

morning   What is more frustrating is I have had to cancel more things due to this sinus thing than I did for my mastectomy.

If you're ever given the choice of a mastectomy or a horrible cold/sinus thing, choose the mastectomy. That's my lesson for May 20, 2019.

PIG PEN

I don't mean as in a sty, I mean the character of Charlie Brown fame. I went for a walk this morning & decided to stroll down the dirt road instead of the paved one. See where this is going? Cars would barrel by leaving a trail of dust which of course soon covered me. All I could think of was Pig Pen walking along trailing dust behind him. That would be me.

Three people have asked in the last couple of days when I was going to update my blog. So, I finally decided to do this & WordPress changed how one adds a post. Nobody consulted me on this modification. Took a few frustrating minutes to figure it out, but I managed.

So....what's new? Jordan is half way through the radiation treatments, Rebecca has a 3-month skin check in July, I have an oncologist appointment coming up in mid-July at which time I will start an injection every 3 months that is supposed to decrease the chance of the breast cancer recurring. I'm not thrilled with an injection because if there is a reaction, one is more or less stuck with it until it wears off.

I just saw I have 15 minutes to get ready to attend a friend's retirement party so I have to scoot. Can't save this as a draft because THAT button is now gone. Grrrr. Juliana's court date is still July 25th; cannot fathom anyone being stupid enough to grant her parent's custody but am very afraid it is possible.

Talk with ya soon.

A COUPLE UPDATES

Thankfully, Rebecca's mole came back clear. Oddly, when their dog went in for the surgery to remove her 'breast' tumor, it had disappeared. (Figures the dog would have that kind of good luck.) The vet had put TJ on antibiotics and now figures the lump was due to an infection which was healed by the drugs. We are thrilled Rebecca is ok and pleased with TJ's results.

We leave Friday for our trip to Ireland, Scotland & Amsterdam. I just can't get excited about this. I think it's due to all the stuff that happened this year; I'm feeling nervous about being gone. I know being here wouldn't change anyone's situation but all the same....

I got up yesterday morning to discover I have a bladder infection. I was able to get into my doctor to get the necessary medications; all I could think was "Thank God this happened now rather than in 3 days when we are overseas.". If you've had a bladder infection, you are aware they can be quite painful. Typically 2 prescriptions are given; one antibiotic and the other a miracle drug that stops the pain. Here's another Public Service Announcement: Do not take pills with ice water. Late yesterday afternoon, I was taking the 'pain eliminator' pill with a glass of water which still had small pieces of ice in it. I got a piece of ice in my mouth & chomped it; I then felt another piece of ice. I chomped down to discover it was the pill. This is a very, very bitter tasting pill which is quite obviously best swallowed whole. In an event, my tongue was numb so I decided to take a look at it. Bright, bright yellow along with my gums & the top of my mouth. I shared this info with my immediate family &

our oldest granddaughter replied "Liver finally failing?"". (I find it disconcerting when they respond with something I would say.) I did call the pharmacist & started the conversation with "This will probably be the stupid question of the day.". I explained what happened & he said there were no problems other than the nasty taste & the odd coloring.

I've packed the bladder pills in my suitcase which looks as if it belongs to a 90+ year old; the regular medications & vitamins, drugs for the bladder infection, back drug #1 in case my back spasms, back drug #2 in case #1 doesn't work, the pills needed in case I get a cold sore, pills used if I can't sleep, cold pills if they are needed, sudafed to take if my ears plug up again, excedrin for possible headaches, bandaids, hydrocortisone cream; I am a traveling drug store.

Now that I think about it, the cold pills, sudafed, excedrin & hydrocortisone cream can probably be easily purchased there as they are all English-speaking countries. Oh well, I'm not unpacking now. When we were in Rome, I tried buying something for shingles (yes, my life can suck) and everything was, as could be expected, in Italian. We attempted talking with a druggist using a translator app but I decided to just be in extreme pain & drink more wine. Before that trip, I had told someone I was taking my own shampoo as I wouldn't be able to read the difference between "hair wash" and "hair remover"; with the shingles, I didn't care to find out if I could decipher the difference between valacyclovir & viagra.

Well, that's enough for today. Do me a favor and remain healthy & safe.

IRELAND/SCOTLAND/ AMSTERDAM

As would be expected, our trip started out with the ramps to Detroit Metro being closed & having to take a detour. It was mostly uneventful from DTW to Boston to Dublin except for the lady sitting next to me got her sandal stuck to the airplane.

Huh? Her sandal stuck to the airplane?? Yes & I loved it! Something I would do but it wasn't me. Along the side of the plane runs – for a lack of a better description – a long cold air vent. She had taken her sandals off & somehow one of the straps slipped into one of the vent slats and would not come out. She's about standing on her head trying to dislodge it & I am dying laughing. I suggested pulling on the vent to see if it would come off & it did – all 12 x 14 inches of it. I told her I didn't know how she was going to walk off the plane with that thing flopping off her shoe but at least she had her sandal.

Arrival to Dublin was more or less uneventful – sort of. Our ATM cards would not work in the ATM's which made it kind of hard to get Euros; we finally found an ATM that would work with my charge card. We then proceeded to the rental car counter to be told our charge cards do not cover rental insurance in Ireland (or Jamaica in case you care), we paid the extra million bucks for insurance & got our tiny rental car & took off for the 5 hour drive to Dingle. Along the way, I used up many international minutes calling the credit union to activate our cards for international travel. Yes, I know to do that ahead of time but was told it was no longer necessary – liars. I also wasted precious minutes confirming with Capital One that they do not provide rental insurance coverage in Ireland (and as if I care, Jamaica).

Enroute to Dingle, we were introduced to somewhat narrow roads but nothing in comparison to what we would find a few days later. In any event, Dingle is a lovely area. We visited a variety of pubs, our favorite being Foxy Johns Hardware & Pub. You can't go wrong; can get the metal & the liquid screwdrivers here. Foxy Johns is definitely a locals pub; some of the people spoke only Gaelic. We ended up at the bar – seating order, as this matters – is Pete, me, an old guy, an old lady, & another old guy around the corner. The lady could speak some English so we managed to chat with all 3 of them. After a bit, the gentleman to my right cupped his hands over his chest & looked at me & pointed to my chest. I told him I'd had cancer & chose a double mastectomy. The lady translated & the man around the corner made the sign of the cross & formed his hands into prayer & I thanked him. Pretty soon, I see this gnarly old finger coming at me & the gentleman sitting next to me started poking my chest. I about fell off my bar stool laughing – I mean really – what the hell! If I still had boobs, I would've knocked his ass off of his stool; I'm not sure why it's ok to poke my boobless chest but WTF. I guess I'm just a walking educational 'poke & prod me' type person.

Our rental car was pumpkin orange. If the car had been bigger, I would have felt like Cinderella. Pretty sad when the inside of the car is smaller than a pumpkin. We kept running into the same couple over & over and she indicated we were hard to miss with that car. They were originally from Michigan but now live in upper New York; ends up she has friends who are friends of my prior neighbor from Pewamo. Go figure.

So, back to the roads. Our stop after Dingle was Galway enroute to the Aran Islands. We took the ferry from somewhere to somewhere else. When we left the ferry, the GPS took us down – seriously – a cow path. We thought for sure the GPS had led us astray but there was a car in front of us and four or five behind us. The dirt road had a strip of grass down the middle & was barely wider than our car. This was NOT a one-way road; it was a two-way road and one needed to move over as far as possible to let an oncoming car through. Ends up that is the typical Irish road outside of the large cities. Holy Mama! As I said, we were the second of 6 cars; the car in front of us pulled over to let an oncoming vehicle pass & ended up dropping a tire into the ditch. We got out of our car & I waved to the people behind us to get out of their vehicles. Few of us spoke the same language but we were able to help out the first car & get them out of the ditch. The United Nations could learn a lot by this example.

Our GPS simply could not locate the B&B in Galway, I called them & we were a block behind them. This B&B was like staying at Grandma's house (not a Grandma like me). Floral furniture, floral bedspreads, crocheted toilet paper cover – really. The lady was sweet as can be; I guess she was what a Grandma is supposed to be like. Oh well....

The Aran Islands are somewhat desolate but worth a day trip. We took a plane over & back as it is much faster than the ferry. For whatever reason, we spent the night at Inishmore (village on the Aran Islands) and really, there is no need to spend the night. If it hadn't been raining, the experience may have been different but I doubt it. We visited a fort which entailed walking through the rain up a rocky path to horribly rocky stairs. A question not answered for me was "How many people have broken their ankle going to/from this fort?".

We then went to Dublin which was o.k. After the quiet of Dingle & Inishmore, it was a little overwhelming. Found the best bar ever in Dingle: The Gin Palace. I thought these women were being served hot tea in a fancy tea pot with fancy cups & saucers. Ended up it was Hendrick's Gin. Women after my own heart.

Ireland is beautiful, very, very green with lots & lots of stone fences that are hundreds of years old. My favorite part? The painted sheep. It was easy painting chipmunks in a trap; I can't fathom running through a field with a spray can of paint coloring the sheep. I could do it; I just can't fathom doing it.

OK, this makes this post long enough. My back has been killing me for the last week. I'm trading it in. I had errands to run today & walked by bras. Every once in a while, it still takes my breath away that I no longer have any use for these. I believe I've handled this very well but there are times I could cry – assuming I ever cried. THEN I walked by dog beds. Of course, I no longer have any use for those either. What a crappy shopping trip!!! I'm having an adult beverage.

SCOTLAND & AMSTERDAM

I loved Edinburgh. Honestly, I would have been tickled pink if someone had offered me the opportunity to walk through the Old Town in a fancy full-hooped dress. The buildings were absolutely gorgeous. Edinburgh Castle is very well done & well worth a visit. And for you historians out there, I do realize that ladies that lived in castles had the more narrow dresses (picture Snow White's step mom) but if I want to pretend to wear a hoopy dress, that's my prerogative.

While the Old Town including the Royal Mile gets all the press, the New Town is also hundreds of years old & well worth a stroll. The Palace of Hollyrood, where the Queen stays while in Scotland, is beautiful.

Near Portree, we discovered many of Scotland's roads are just like Ireland's – little more than cow paths. It didn't matter which of us was driving; whoever was in the passenger seat had the worst seat in the car. I clenched my jaw so tight, I cracked a tooth. We made it to St. Andrews & were able to walk the course on Sunday. It was, of course, rainy & windy but it was enjoyable to see the course & the beautiful buildings near it.

We did try a small amount of haggis & it was surprisingly delicious.

When we returned our rental car in Scotland, the little punk taking in the cars insisted we had damaged the bottom. He was literally laying on the ground looking under the car. We insisted we had not damaged it. The guy at the counter asked if we'd looked at the car before taking it; who in the world lays on the ground & looks under a rental car? I'd suggest you start doing it. Anyway, we were getting nowhere with them, had a flight to catch to Amsterdam & I told Pete we'd deal with it when we got home.

Ended up, we'd have had plenty of time to argue with him as our flight was delayed four hours. We arrived in Amsterdam after dark & had no idea how to get to our B&B. At this point, I told Pete I am starting to see the benefit of group tours. We knew we had to take the train from the airport to downtown Amsterdam; of course, the kiosks don't take foreign credit cards so we had to wait in line to get a ticket for the train. Upon arriving in Amsterdam (dark & raining), I said we are just getting a cab. We found a cab & were dropped off on the street of our B&B as it was blocked for traffic. The cab driver said "Just walk down the street, you'll see it.". Yup, we saw it & hauled our stuff up 3 flights of stairs; these were spiral stairs, very narrow spiral stairs but we had a fantastic view of a canal.

Amsterdam is a very cool city & the Anne Frank House is a must-see. It is a very sad reminder of a horrible time in the world.

It's relatively easy to walk through the town as long as you watch out for trams, cars, scooters, motorcycles & bikes. It's a tad dangerous; over here when a walk light is blinking 10, it means you have 10 seconds to cross the road. In Amsterdam, a light blinking 10 means you have 10 seconds BEFORE you can cross the road. One hell of a difference! Didn't need to learn that lesson twice!!! Of course, we went to the Red Light District; why do you even wonder? We went through The Sex Museum which basically proved there's been perverts in this world since at least the 16th century. And speak of pervs, we saw them walk into & out of the prostitutes' rooms. Whole different world; well, for some of us, it's a whole different world.

On about our 3rd day in Amsterdam, my cracked tooth was throbbing. They do not sell tooth-numbing stuff in Amsterdam. I told Pete my tooth hurt worse than my mastectomy.

Overall, it was a very good trip; although I am totally sick of clouds & rain. A few things other than the roads that we found the 3 countries have in common: There is no top sheet, there are no screens on the windows, there are lots of flying bugs that like to come into your room, many buildings do not have elevators, none of the B&B's we stayed at had A/C, only 2 B&B's had fans, bacon is fatty thin-sliced ham, bread is a staple for breakfast along with stuff such as baked beans, blood sausage, & tomatoes. I have a list of items to bring on 'foreign' vacations; I've added a sheet, a fly swatter, & tooth-numbing gel. I'm willing to share that list should you want it.

VICHY SHOWER

This experience was a few years back but I felt it is worth sharing.

I had a coupon for a local business and could choose from a variety of options including pedicures, facials, body treatments, and a vichy shower experience. Since I've done several of the others, I opted to try the vichy shower. Allow me to share.

I was introduced to the masseuse who would be doing the treatment – let's make it simple and call her Jane Doe. The first step is Jane places about 7 cards face-down on a table. I thought maybe she was going to tell my fortune but I was instructed to pick 3 cards based on the words on the card. She then linked the choices to scents; all of which were unpleasant. She asked which one I wanted & I told her my preference would be none. She looked so crest-fallen, I chose the least offensive one.

There is a door leading to the vichy shower room which has maybe a 6" space between the outer door & a solid glass door. I was instructed Jane would step out of the room & I was to remove all clothing & put on a robe. The 6" space was to store my purse, shoes, clothes, etc. Easy enough.

In the 'vichy room', the floor, ceiling, and walls are all tiled and there are metal spigots hanging from the ceiling; the bed is smack-dab in the middle of the room under the spigots. On the wall, there is what can only be called a small fire hose – about ½ the size of those that are in office buildings. It had gauges which added to the fire hose look. The overall feel? Actually, that of a dimly lit operating room. I started wondering what I'd gotten myself into. Jane comes back and says she will go mix up a salt scrub and that I should disrobe and climb onto the table and cover myself with the large towel. I am 5'8"; I had a hard time getting on that table. Anyone shorter would need a small ladder or a large step stool. So, I get snuggled onto the bed, covered with the warm towel – so far, so good. That's when I notice there are drains along the entire length of the table. Operating bed? I think not, it's a freakin' autopsy table. Remember all of the tile in the room? No one would be able to hear me scream & clean-up would be a breeze.

Jane comes back in and starts the second step which is to squirt the client with oil & to literally shake on a salt scrub. I felt like a huge butt roast. After the salt scrub is applied, Jane again steps out of the room indicating she needs to change her clothes. I was expecting the room to soon get around 350 degrees. A short time later, the room temperature had not increased and Jane comes back into the room. She has changed into gym shorts & a t-shirt; she proceeds to put on a swimming cap & a large pair of goggles. I was looking for the chain saw as I'm pretty sure I've seen this on "Dexter".

So, our Ms. Doe begins the 3rd step which starts the hose. Holy crap! It was like a giant power washer – I kid you not. I've seen paint come off boards when using a power washer; I said a quick prayer for my skin. Ms. Doe started on my feet & actually, I honestly admit, it didn't feel too bad. Part way through, I'm thinking I might recommend this to friends. Then she got by my shoulders. I don't like to snorkel – I was wishing I had one though. Mountains of water run down your face onto the floor. Gallons & gallons of water, it is indescribable. I could breathe but couldn't see. Water was running through my ears into my brain. The entire experience is with the client face down; they also use the hose to spray water between the front of you & the table; I swear, I was floating a couple times. I was quickly becoming a non-fan of the vichy shower.

After what seemed like hours, Jane put away the fire hose & begins step 4 which turns on the overhead spigots one-by-one. The spigots start at your lower spine and go up to your head. OK – stick with me here – a few years ago, Pete & I were enjoying Gizzard Fest in Potterville when there was a tornado warning. My spouse inexplicably decided we'd go to the car rather than into a packed building. Running through the pelting hail and rain with 70 mph winds does not compare with the vichy shower spigots. Prior to this point, I was thinking I couldn't possibly get any wetter, I was wrong. Jane asked me how I felt, my only honest response I could give was "clean". My fingers were wrinkled, I'd have to assume the same of my toes. With all the water in my eyes, I couldn't see them. The final step is an application of lotion, which if it hadn't stunk, would have been fine. I have to admit my skin was baby-smooth; any dead cells had been sand-blasted away in the treatment. Would I do this again? Hell no!

When looked up on the internet, descriptions include "feels delicious", "relax the entire body" "relax in your cocoon". I liked the warning that 'your hair may get wet'. After > 24 hours, mine still isn't dry! I highly recommend sticking with the old-fashioned massages and leaving the vichy shower for the seals.

WELL, GEE WHILICKERS

Our grandson, Noah, has been working extremely hard to make the 9th grade basketball team. Last week, it was discovered he had broken his leg down by the ankle bone. He then went to a sports doctor who indicated that was an old break but he definitely has soft tissue damage which is causing the pain & inability to run or jump. Poor kid, he was so hoping to make the team. Tryouts are this week. I feel horrible for him.

Our great-grandson Harrison had another seizure this week (2nd in 5 months) so is on epilepsy medication for at least 2 years.

My back has been horrific & I have another MRI Friday morning.

I'd like to make a joke but it just isn't in me. Well, maybe...... other family members have had illnesses over the last few months & my sister Rita indicated that when she leaves this world, she will have "...a straight path through those golden gates.". I asked her if she was going to McDonald's; she said "Who?". Anyway, she finally figured it out. I then had to remind her it is the Pearly Gates not the Golden Gates so she will probably spend her spiritual world haunting San Francisco.

THANKFUL FOR....

I will get to that in a minute. Right now allow me to share I am typing this while stoned out of my gourd. My back has been excruciatingly painful for weeks; another MRI showed the same things: bone marrow edema, arthritis, disc issues blah blah blah. I asked my doctor for a muscle relaxer that perhaps won't make me as sleepy & she prescribed me something or other. She said to take one & if that doesn't work, take another. So, after another night of not sleeping because my back hurts, I got up this morning and took two of them at the same time on an empty stomach. Holy shit, I am flying. I was going to go downstairs to exercise but I think it might be dangerous to go down the steps right now plus I'm not sure I'd remember what to do when I got down there. Probably drool. Yes, I know to be careful with muscle relaxers; I've taken them off & on for years for neck or back pain and I now know not to do two at the same time. I

am thankful for being able to still learn new things

All kidding aside, I am beyond grateful that Rebecca, Jordan, & I have recuperated from our bouts with cancer & pray every night none of us have a recurrence. I am grateful for the family & friends in our lives. I am thankful to wake up every day; I am thankful to live in a free country; I am thankful for muscle relaxers. (Re-read my first paragraph, second sentence.) We need to be at my Mom's by 1:00; I hope I'm able to shower before then or I am showing up in my exercise clothes & morning hair.

Wishes to everyone for a wonderful Thanksgiving Day.

I'M GIVING UP....

....drinking part time and taking it up full time. What a painful month! Almost every movement makes my back spasm; I'm getting a tad cranky. I started PT on Tuesday but he couldn't work on my back because whenever he touched the area that needs to be worked on, my back would spasm & I'd curl into a fetal position. I've gone back to doing the basic back stretches & it is slowly getting better but has a long way to go.

Saturday night was especially great because as I went through my nightly ritual of getting up to urinate, I couldn't get off the toilet because my back was spasming. I was hotter than hell & could only see dots. I contemplated yelling for Pete but all I wanted to do was somehow get to the cold floor. Anyways, Pete finally figured out I'd been gone too long & came into the bathroom to discover I couldn't move. Who in the hell signed me up for this stuff anyways? We finally made our way into the living room & I stood against the glass slider to cool down; Pete is pretty sure he saw steam coming off the window. Once I was able to walk again, we scrounged through the prescription cabinet for the pain pills provided to me a couple of years ago; these cannot be taken with a muscle relaxer.

Sunday night, I took one of the special pills; my back spasmed anytime I even moved an arm (thankfully I only have 2 arms, I feel bad for an octopus with back spasms. Does an octopus even have a back?). My back was a tad better Monday morning. I took the same pill Monday night; I do not like to take these as I do not want to wake up dead. Plus they can't be taken with alcohol; who develops these things, anyways? Tuesday night I was back to the regular muscle relaxer; last night, I think was the same. These things make me so groggy I can't remember a thing. Tonight, I'm going back to my special cookies.

Our oldest granddaughter, Alicia, asked on Tuesday if I could watch the boys Wednesday so she could take the dog to the vet. Pete had a dentist appointment so couldn't go along & I told her I didn't think I could lift the boys but I could drive the dog to the vet. Sorry to use the word again – but what in the HELL was I thinking? If you haven't already seen the Allstate Mayhem commercial where the guy is the dog, you need to see it. That was me & Sandy. Not really, she behaved pretty well in the car; it was walking her to & from the vet that was darned near impossible because she pulls on the leash. When we got back to Alicia's, I had her get the mutt out of my car.

And speaking of being at Alicia's....when I returned from the vet, Marshall wanted orange juice & they were all out. I told him I'd go to the store & get some for him; he also wanted a "brown" donut. They were out of the chocolate glazed ones so I purchased a chocolate one with chocolate frosting. I return, put the donut on a plate & present it to the discerning toddler. He pointed out that the frosting was wrinkled in one spot so I smoothed it out. There were two more spots that were 'wrinkled' so I also smoothed those out. At the 4th one, I turned the damn donut upside down. He then pointed out frosting was coming through the hole. I finally told him to just eat it & he did with no fuss. I think the little turd was trying to see how far he could push me.

Today (Thursday, 12/5), I had two appointments at the U of M to discuss the issues I am having with the non-HRT therapy. You do NOT want the details. In any event, we have Plan 1 and if that doesn't work over the next 4 months, we will try Plan 2. I will be honest here & say I am feeling frustrated, aggravated, annoyed, angry, displeased, bothered – get the picture? As always, I know it could be worse & I pray I never have to say I'd like to go back to this rather than whatever I may face later. But enough already!!!

I will close this out by stating I am very, very impressed with the staff at U of M's breast cancer center. They are kind, understanding, patient, & willing to refer you to a colleague for help, I am very pleased to be a patient there – well, that sounds stupid, who in the hell is pleased to be a patient anywhere? In any event, if I have to be treated for breast cancer & it's lingering side-effects, I am glad it is at the U of M.

Made in the USA
Monee, IL
29 June 2020